More Praise for

The Hamster Revolution
for Meetings

"Overwhelmed by meetings? Double your productivity with this fast, fun, and effective read."
—Marshall Goldsmith, author of *What Got You Here Won't Get You There*

"Practical, powerful, and easy to apply!"
—Betsy Myers, Chief Operating Officer, Barack Obama Presidential Campaign

"Take control of meetings and get more done!"
—Jack Forestell, Vice President of Marketing and Analytics, Capital One Financial

"A must-read business book! Grow your productivity, network, and career with these bold, new meeting techniques."
—Keith Ferrazzi, author of *Never Eat Alone*

"Loved it! Effective meetings and a ton of time saved. Brilliant!'
—Beth Behnke, Director, Human Resources, Venoco, Inc.

"Go green! Boost virtual meeting results and reduce your carbon footprint!"
—Gus Kellogg, Chief Executive Officer, Greenleaf Biofuels

"Real-world meeting ideas that reclaim time and increase your treasure."
—Garry Ridge, CEO and President, WD-40 Company

The Hamster
Revolution
for Meetings

How to Meet Less
and Get More Done

The Hamster
Revolution

for Meetings

Mike Song
Vicki Halsey
Tim Burress

BK

Berrett–Koehler Publishers, Inc.
San Francisco
a BK Business book

Berrett-Koehler Publishers, Inc.
235 Montgomery Street, Suite 650
San Francisco, CA 94104-2916
Tel: (415) 288-0260   Fax: (415) 362-2512   www.bkconnection.com

Ordering Information

Quantity sales Special discounts are available on quantity purchases by corporations, associations, and others. For details, contact the "Special Sales Department" at the Berrett-Koehler address above.

Individual sales Berrett-Koehler publications are available through most bookstores. They can also be ordered directly from Berrett-Koehler: Tel: (800) 929-2929; Fax: (802) 864-7626; www. bkconnection.com

Orders for college textbook/course adoption use Please contact Berrett-Koehler: Tel: (800) 929-2929; Fax: (802) 864-7626.

Orders by U.S. trade bookstores and wholesalers Please contact Ingram Publisher Services, Tel: (800) 509-4887; Fax: (800) 838-1149; E-mail: customer.service@ingrampublisherservices.com; or visit www.ingrampublisherservices.com/Ordering for details about electronic ordering.

Berrett-Koehler and the BK logo are registered trademarks of Berrett-Koehler Publishers, Inc.

Printed in the United States of America

Berrett-Koehler books are printed on long-lasting acid-free paper. When it is available, we choose paper that has been manufactured by environmentally responsible processes. These may include using trees grown in sustainable forests, incorporating recycled paper, minimizing chlorine in bleaching, or recycling the energy produced at the paper mill.

Library of Congress Cataloging-in-Publication Data

Song, Mike, 1964-
   The hamster revolution for meetings : how to meet less and get more done / Mike Song,
       Vicki Halsey, Tim Burress.
     p. cm. -- (The hamster revolution for meetings)
   Includes bibliographical references and index.
   ISBN 978-1-60509-007-8 (alk. paper)
   1. Corporate meetings. 2. Industrial productivity. I. Halsey, Vicki, 1955- II. Burress, Tim,
       1964- III. Title.
   HD2743.S66 2009
   658.4'56--dc22
                            2009015691

First Edition
14 13 12 11 10   10 9 8 7 6 5 4 3 2

Book Producer: Tolman Creek Design LLC, Copy Editor: Merrilee Eggleston, Indexer: Shan Young

Mike Song

For Mom and Dad. Your amazing love, inspiration, insight, and sacrifice will shine forever in my heart.

Vicki Halsey

For my precious Rick, Nick, and Jake and my transformative Blanchard family.

Tim Burress

In memory of George. Thanks for your simple words of wisdom and never-ending laughter.

Contents

Foreword
Ken Blanchard

Forty-three percent.

That's the amount of time professionals say they waste during meetings. It's a stunning number when you consider that meetings consume a huge chunk of every business day.

Making the most of meeting time may be the greatest opportunity we have to get more done, be happier in our jobs, and free up more time. And given the challenges our world faces right now, meetings that identify and solve real problems would go a long way toward making things better. Yet ever since people began gathering together to get work done, the world has been plagued by meetings without clear agendas, meetings that stray off course, meetings with incomplete action items, and meetings without accountability and follow-through.

The Hamster Revolution for Meetings excites me because the authors not only provide sound advice on how to manage traditional, face-to-face meetings, they also show how much easier meetings can be with the help of technology: e-calendars, virtual meeting tools, PDAs, and more. Plus, it's a fun story that gets to the point. You can read it cover-to-cover during a 90-minute plane ride.

If you're like the average professional, you spend more than a quarter of your day in meetings. Assuming you want to be a great leader or team player, don't you think it's a good idea to have a strategy for making the most of every meeting you attend? There's no question that this book will save you time—but it also just might take you, your company, and our world to a higher level.

—Ken Blanchard,
coauthor of *The One Minute Manager*®
and *Leading at a Higher Level*

1

STUCK!

We were stuck.

Kim, our flight attendant, had just informed us that a violent thunderstorm was rapidly rolling in.

"If we get seated quickly, we'll be able to take off a few minutes early and miss the bad weather," she said.

Unfortunately, one final passenger was arriving at the last possible minute, spoiling the plan. Everyone was grumbling and straining to see who it was.

"Uh, welcome aboard!" said Kim, sounding confused. She was talking to someone, but from our vantage point, no one appeared to be there.

What was going on?

Kim turned to watch the invisible passenger trudge down the aisle. At the front of the plane, heads turned and people gasped.

"Did you see that?"

"Oh my!"

Straining to see, I leaned into the aisle to get a better look. Suddenly I was face-to-face with an attractive yet extremely frazzled female hamster. She was no more than two feet tall and wore a dark blue business suit.

My fellow passengers were stunned. The plane fell silent.

"Hi, I'm Iris," she gasped. "I just ran all the way through the airport."

A shocked-looking businessman across the aisle said, "You're a...a..."

"Late, I know," said Iris apologetically as she motioned to the empty seat next to me. "That's mine."

After stowing her computer case, she hopped into her seat and buckled in.

Iris seemed to sense the stares of her fellow passengers.

"Sorry everyone, I was in a meeting that ran way over," she announced tersely. "And my twins, it's their birthday tomorrow and I had to make this flight."

Kim reviewed the safety instructions as our plane backed slowly away from the gate.

Glancing over at Iris, I said, "Meetings can suck the life out of you."

"Tell me about it," she replied. "This one was *hideous*."

"How so?"

"It was a presentation to some of our top execs for a major productivity initiative—the most important thing I've ever worked on."

"So what went wrong?" I asked.

"Everything," groaned Iris. "It started late and veered into total chaos. David, my assistant, couldn't get the LCD projector working and no one wanted to follow the agenda."

She looked up, shut her eyes, and grimaced as if she was replaying every painful minute in her mind.

"This was a productivity project?"

"Operation Elevation," said Iris sarcastically as she glanced out the window. "We're transitioning 500 colleagues from our corporate headquarters to home offices in order to eliminate commute time and building costs."

"I've heard about this," I said thoughtfully. "You're improving work/life balance, boosting productivity, *and* helping the environment. Don't they call it home-sourcing?"

Iris gave a glum nod. "The benefits are endless. If we do it right, we save over $10 million a year. If we do it wrong—and our people can't adapt—we lose millions!"

"Feeling a bit of pressure?" I asked.

"A *ton* of pressure," corrected Iris. "My stomach's been in knots for weeks."

"And today's meeting was critical?"

"Yes," said Iris. "It was my first meeting with the top brass. I was so excited when the CEO picked me to lead the team."

She let out a heavy sigh.

"Now it feels like Operation Quicksand! It was supposed to take my career to the next level—not bury it. If our next meeting is anything like this one, I'm pretty sure they'll replace me."

For a moment Iris seemed lost in her thoughts as she stared out the window. Storm clouds were rolling in from the west.

"What exactly do you do, Iris?" I asked.

"National sales manager at Spex Media," she replied. "We design and deliver large multimedia events for product launches."

Iris turned toward me with a slightly suspicious look. "You sure ask a lot of questions. What do *you* do for a living?"

"Sorry for prying. I'm a productivity coach—I help busy people get more done."

Iris looked skeptical. "How?"

"For example, I help them *get control* of meetings."

"Hah!" said Iris, dismissing the idea with a wave of her paw. "We tried that. We had a big meeting initiative last year. All our managers went off-site for a two-day training session." She gestured thumbs down. "None of it stuck."

"Why?"

"I'm not sure. Perhaps there was too much information. Maybe we didn't focus enough on what the facilitator was saying.

"We made all these big plans. But when we got back to the office there were mountains of email and overdue projects. The whole thing wasn't very…"

"Practical?" I suggested.

"Yup," said Iris. "And it didn't mesh with the way we work. Spex meetings have *changed* in the past few years."

"How?"

"They're less formal and more virtual," said Iris. "We do lots of teleconferences, and most of the stuff we learned didn't apply to virtual meetings. Also, our leaders didn't have time to create elaborate agendas or establish ground rules at every meeting."

"Did it help you reduce unnecessary time spent in meetings?"

Iris laughed. "No way. We're meeting more than ever and getting less and less done."

She closed her eyes and put her head in her paws. "It's hopeless. Operation Elevation is a mess and I'm doomed to run from one chaotic, dead-end meeting to another like a, a…"

She paused and gave me an exasperated look.

"Hamster on a wheel?" I offered.

"That's it!" cried Iris, bolting up in her seat. "It's like I'm running in place and never getting anything accomplished. And when I'm in a meeting, I often feel like I'm trapped in a, a…"

"Hamster cage?"

"Yes!" she exclaimed. She lowered her voice and whispered, "I'm sick of feeling like a hamster *all* the time."

It occurred to me that Iris had no idea she had actually morphed into a hamster. Perhaps the transformation had been so gradual she hadn't noticed.

The plane hesitated on the runway.

The pilot announced, "We're going to be delayed a bit longer since we didn't get that early start. It looks like the storm may pass to the north, but traffic control is asking us to wait a few more minutes."

Several passengers groaned and some even glared at Iris. She slumped in her seat.

"Look, Iris," I said. "Since we're going to be sitting here for a while, maybe I can help you with your meeting challenge."

Iris looked around as if she was searching for another place to sit.

"I appreciate it—but as I said, we're hopeless."

She glanced out the rain-streaked window and sighed. "It wasn't supposed to be like this."

"What do you mean?" I asked.

"My career—my life," she replied. "I always pictured this amazing job where people worked together and achieved a ton each day."

"What did you think your meetings would be like?" I asked.

Her whiskers twitched as she considered. "For some reason I thought that each meeting would have a clear purpose, structure, and a set of follow-up actions that people would complete before the next meeting. I guess I saw them as places where people energized each other and did their best thinking. You know—got fired up and charged forward with renewed focus. I pictured myself coming home to my husband and the twins feeling relaxed and satisfied that I had contributed and accomplished a lot."

Shaking her head sadly, Iris added, "I never thought I'd spend my days running from one lousy meeting to the next, feeling like a stressed-out hamster!"

2

LIFTOFF

Iris turned to me. "I hope I didn't offend you…by saying that I didn't need help with meetings."

"Oh no," I replied. "I understand completely."

She fidgeted in her seat for a moment.

"I've noticed lately—there's a lot more *leg room* on these flights."

"There sure is," I agreed, smiling gently. Iris was quiet for a moment.

Suddenly she asked, "How exactly do you help people with meetings?"

I smiled again. "At first, you may think my approach is a bit odd."

"No I won't," said Iris emphatically. "I promise."

"Okay," I said. "If you feel like a hamster on a wheel—running harder and faster but getting nowhere—that's a serious problem. You need more than just a few tips and tricks to reclaim your life."

"Sounds reasonable," encouraged Iris.

"We need a whole new way to meet, something revolutionary. And the good news is that this revolution has already begun. It's taking off around the world and anyone can join."

"Does this movement have a name?" she asked, raising her eyebrows.

"The Hamster Revolution for Meetings."

I heard some snickers from behind us. Apparently, other passengers were eavesdropping.

"Ridiculous name," said one with a smirk.

"But keep talking, we're drowning in meetings too!" grinned another.

Iris continued. "What's involved with," she formed quotation marks with her paws, "*joining?*"

"For starters, you make a commitment to be responsible for the value of meetings you both run *and* attend. Then you master a new set of meeting tools and share them with other hamsters."

"So it's a productivity cult for rodents," said Iris with a wicked grin.

"People join because they're sick and tired of feeling trapped in the meeting cage," I explained. "It's an escape plan that helps you reclaim your life and get more done."

Her grin disappeared and she looked wistful. "A day full of useless meetings can really be exhausting. And then I have to stay late to catch up on assignments and email. That's why my family hates me these days."

"So meetings are messing up things at home?"

"Uh huh," said Iris resignedly. "How is your approach different from the training we had last year?"

"There are huge differences," I said. "Instead of teaching you everything under the sun, we focus on your *five biggest meeting pain points*—the ones that are causing 80 percent of the problems."

She seemed to approve of this approach. "So I don't have to spend two whole days becoming a meeting goddess?"

I shook my head and continued, "And this revolution isn't just for leaders. As I said, everyone must contribute to the effectiveness of meetings."

Iris thought for a moment. "That makes sense. These days everyone on our team both schedules and attends meetings—it's not just a leader thing."

"Exactly," I said. "And this revolution is designed for the information age. It's all about the way information flows through your meetings and the technology we use to plan, schedule, and follow up. That's why they call me an *info coach* rather than a meeting coach."

Just then the captain came on. "There's an opening in the storm, folks, and we're finally cleared for liftoff." Our jet began to move down the runway, slowly gathering momentum.

"So you think you can help me?"

"I know I can," I said confidently.

"And this hamster thing—which frankly sounds too good to be true—will save me time?" she asked, raising her voice over the revving jet engines. We were rocketing forward, gathering momentum.

"Fifteen days a year!" I said loudly. "And we'll get Operation Elevation *and* your life back on track."

Iris thought for a moment as the jet neared liftoff speed.

"Do I have to sign anything?" she asked with a cautious smile.

"No," I laughed, "but you do have to commit to making every meeting better than the last."

"I guess I could do that," she said in a tone that still conveyed some doubt. Then she brightened. "Okay, Coach, I'll join!"

She raised a tiny fist into the air and cried, "Go hamsters!"

There was a smattering of applause and laughter from our fellow passengers as the big jet rose off the runway, powering its way into the sky. A moment later we broke through the clouds and suddenly the cabin was filled with sunlight.

We were finally on our way.

3

THE BIG FIVE

After the jet reached cruising altitude, Iris pulled a small bag of celery sticks from her computer case.

"Been craving veggies lately," she said between munches. "So what are the five big meeting *pain points* you've been yammering about?"

"Why don't you tell me?" I replied. "What bothers you most about meetings at Spex?"

Iris thought for a moment and said, "Sheer volume. We meet too much."

"What else?"

"Our meetings always start and end late—we jokingly call that 'Spex Time.' We never stay on track, agendas are rare, and presentations run way too long."

Her whiskers twitched as she paused to think. "Oh yes, and action items *vaporize* the moment people leave."

"Does this happen in both live and virtual meetings?" I asked.

Iris rolled her eyes. "Don't get me started on virtual meetings! Most of them are boring as mud. I swear that half of my team is doing email during our weekly sales managers' teleconference—especially Alex."

"Alex?" I asked.

"He's one of our best regional sales managers. But he never says a word in meetings, and if I call on him, he always sounds startled. He's probably surfing the web or downloading music."

Iris leaned toward me and whispered, "Personally, I'm starting to wonder if he really exists."

"Okay," I laughed. "What other concerns do you have about virtual meetings?"

"Tech issues," she said. "In today's Operation Elevation meeting, the senior leadership team had trouble logging in to the web conference, so we started 15 minutes late. In other remote meetings—often with our clients—we've had computers freeze, noisy cell phones, dropped lines, scheduling problems, you name it."

"So virtual meetings are a big concern?"

"They could save Spex millions in travel costs and help us go green," sighed Iris. "Unfortunately, our virtual meetings stink!"

She flashed a desperate, defeated look. "Can you untangle this mess?"

"Sure we can," I said, reaching into my computer bag. I handed Iris a small bifold card titled *The Hamster Revolution for Meetings Power Tools*. "We start here," I said, pointing to the first section of the card, "The Hamster Revolution Meeting Plan."

"Neat," said Iris, looking carefully at the card. "You've outlined most of the challenges I just mentioned and provided a solution for each one."

| The Hamster Revolution Meeting Plan ||
Challenge	Solution
1. **Meeting Overload**	POSE the right questions and cut meeting time by 15%
2. **Missing Key Elements**	The Meeting Power Draft locks in key success ingredients.
3. **Virtual Meeting Chaos**	Two checklists make remote meetings riveting *and* glitch free.
4. **Meandering Meetings**	The NNNO tool keeps meetings on track—every time.
5. **Incomplete Action Items**	A Meeting Action Plan (MAP) helps everyone complete action items.

"We've also found that the top five meeting complaints apply to many *different* kinds of meetings, including staff, brainstorming, one-on-one, and client meetings."

"So addressing these five problems helps almost everyone in almost every meeting situation," reasoned Iris, taking the card from my hand and leaning back in her seat to study it.

"We're experiencing all of these challenges," she said. "But how long does this hamster thing take?"

I pointed at the plan and said, "We can cover the first two items, Meeting Overload and Missing Key Elements, on this short flight.

"If you find our discussion valuable and want to learn more, I'll attend a few of your virtual meetings and provide feedback and solutions next week—that's how we'll tackle Virtual Meeting Chaos.

"Finally, I'd be happy to visit you and your team at Spex headquarters in three weeks. That's when we'll cover the last two topics, Meandering Meetings and Incomplete Action Items. Your total time investment will be three hours."

"Not bad. But what about those 15 days?" asked Iris, with a mischievous grin that said *prove it to me*. "How can you possibly save me that much time?"

I smiled and said, "I thought you'd never ask."

4

WHERE DID MY LIFE GO?

I handed Iris a calculator and asked, "How much time do you spend in meetings each year?"

Iris shrugged. "I have no idea."

"Well, let's find out!" I said. "Look at your e-calendar for the past four weeks and figure out the average number of meetings you attended each day."

Iris pulled out her laptop and took a moment to add up her meetings.

"I'm averaging 3.3 meetings a day," she said.

"Now multiply 3.3 by the average duration of your meetings. This will tell us how much time you spend in meetings each day."

"I would say our average meeting lasts 60 minutes." Iris typed in the numbers. "And that means I spend roughly 200 minutes per day in meetings."

"Okay, now multiply 200 minutes times 240 business days per year."

Iris did the calculation and mused, "Wow. That's 48,000 minutes per year!"

I nodded. "Now divide by 60 to convert those meeting minutes into hours."

Iris tapped in the numbers and looked surprised. She held up the calculator. "I spend 800 hours in meetings each year?"

"Now divide 800 by 8 hours to get the total number of continuous eight-hour days you spend in meetings each year."

Iris was stunned. "I spend 100 days a year in meetings!"

I nodded enthusiastically. "Now, just for fun, multiply your 100 days by the percentage of meeting time that you feel is wasted."

"At least a third," said Iris quickly—she didn't need a calculator this time. She slumped in her seat pretending to faint. Opening her eyes she said, "You've got to be kidding. I'm wasting 33 days a year on meetings? That can't be right."

She punched in the numbers again and came to the same conclusion. Iris thought for a moment and then tapped in one more set of numbers and held up the calculator.

"There are roughly a thousand employees at Spex who probably waste just as much time as I do in meetings. SO WE'RE WASTING 33,000 DAYS A YEAR!"

Iris looked shell-shocked. She handed me the calculator and I typed in a few numbers.

"At an average wage of $30 per hour—"

Iris plugged her ears. "I don't want to hear it!"

"Spex is wasting—"

"Blah, blah, blah I can't hear you!"

"Over seven million dollars a year."

Iris picked up an air sickness bag. "I think I'm going to need this! Stop the hamster wheel—I want to get off!"

Passengers all around us burst out laughing.

"Seriously, Iris," I said. "Our research, from more than 20,000 surveys, demonstrates that the time wasted in meetings in the U.S. alone is over a half trillion dollars per year." [1]

"Yuck," groaned Iris. Then her expression changed from disgust to determination.

"Okay, Coach, you've made your point. Meetings are out of control. So let's hear some solutions!"

I raised my hand. "Whoa, not so fast!"

"Uh oh," smirked Iris, raising one eyebrow. "Are you going to ask me for money? I knew this was too good to be true."

"No!" I laughed. "First, we need to figure out what to do with all the time you'll save. Our objective is to reduce your meeting time by 15 percent."

"And 15 percent of 100 days spent in meetings is 15 days," reasoned Iris.

"One basic tenet of the Hamster Revolution is that we always channel the time we save into important, life-changing projects," I said.

"I guess that's smarter than scheduling more meetings," agreed Iris.

"Fifteen days a year equates to 30 minutes a day. How could you use that time? Can you think of two goals—one personal and one professional?"

Iris pondered my request. "Hmmm. What could I do with 15 days?"

"You decide," I urged. "But once you select your goals, write them down."

She thought for a moment. Then she opened a document and began typing out her goals:

My Hamster Revolution Meeting Goals

Personal: *Volunteer to coach the twins' soccer team this summer.*

Professional: *Make Operation Elevation a success and deliver three major productivity initiatives that help Spex drive sales and profit by year-end.*

Iris and I discussed her goals. Then she opened a folder on her laptop that was filled with family photos. She had beautiful pictures of her husband, Peter, and their twin 11-year-old daughters.

The twins, Erin and Grace, had been getting into a bit of trouble at school. Iris and Peter were trying to spend more time with them. They were growing up fast and needed a lot of attention and love.

With her goals in mind, Iris was ready to plan her escape from the meeting cage.

5

THE ART OF MEETING LESS

"Hey, Iris," I asked. "Do you find it hard to turn down a meeting invitation?"

"Kind of," she said.

"What's the first thing you do when someone sends you an invitation?"

"I check my calendar."

"Here's something I'd like you to check *before* you look at your calendar," I said, pointing to The Hamster Revolution for Meetings Power Tools card.

"The POSE Meeting Reduction Tool?" asked Iris.

"If you want to meet less, you have to POSE the right questions before agreeing to a meeting. POSE is an acronym that will remind you to ask some important questions:

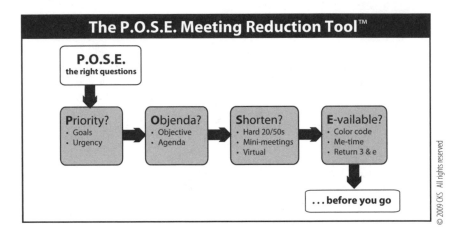

1. **"P is for Priority**. Does this meeting relate to my top goals for the year?
2. **"O is for Objenda™**. Does this meeting have a clearly stated objective and agenda?
3. **"S is for Shorten**. Can we cut the time we spend attending and scheduling meetings?
4. **"E is for E-vailable™**. Are we effectively using our e-calendars to accurately reflect available times?"

Iris frowned. "You're going to have to explain each one."

P—Is It a Priority?

"Okay," I said. "From now on, the first question to POSE when invited to a meeting is *Is this meeting a priority?*"

"But I do that," protested Iris.

"Really?" I asked. "What are your top 10 priority goals for this year?"

Iris looked flustered. "Well, uh, I have an overall sales goal and we're trying to hire three salespeople and, oh yes, Operation Elevation is certainly at the top of the list."

"List?" I asked. "So you have a document that summarizes your goals? Something you could open in a couple seconds?"

"Well, no," said Iris, frowning at her computer. "What does this have to do with meetings?"

"When considering meeting requests, we tend to focus on *availability* at the expense of priority. A handy list of your high-priority goals provides an easy way to filter out low-priority requests."

"I get it," said Iris. "It's not just the list of goals—it's being able to quickly find that list when a meeting is proposed."

"Preferably in just one mouse click," I added. "Take a look at this."

I opened my laptop and clicked on an icon on the left side of my lower horizontal toolbar. A spreadsheet immediately popped open, revealing my top 10 goals for the year. Iris' eyes lit up.

"Cool," she said, studying my document with care. "Let me create my own version."

She turned to her laptop and got to work. In a few minutes she had a rough draft of her goals.

"One question," said Iris, pointing at my computer screen. "How did you get this shortcut icon into your lower toolbar?"

"It's easy," I said. "Here's how you do it:

1. "Surf to the Goals document within My Documents.

2. "Click and drag the document to the left-hand side of your lower horizontal toolbar (also known as the Quick Launch bar). You may need to right-click on the lower toolbar to make sure there is no check mark next to Lock the Taskbar."

Iris' Top 10 Goals for This Year			
Objective: Achieve $42 million in sales			
Priority	When	Project	Progress
1	Q1	Design & launch campaign to develop $10 million in new business	Medium
2	Q1	Launch customer appreciation program to increase repeat sales	Low
3	Q2	Successfully implement Operation Elevation	Low
4	Q3	Hire 3 talented salespeople	Strong
5	Q2	Develop 2 team-building initiatives	Medium
6	Q1 and 3	Hold 2 Sales Team Plan of Action Meetings (Jan. and June)	Strong
7	Q4	Streamline and improve New Hire Training Manual	Low
8	Q2	Improve sales incentive plan	Strong
9	Q3	Improve online customer service web page	Low
10	Q4	Explore new lead generation options	Medium

Visit the info center at infoexcellence.com to download a free blank copy of the goals spreadsheet.

Iris completed the maneuver in less than 10 seconds.

"Terrific," I said, pointing at Iris' e-calendar. "Take a look at last month's meetings and compare them with your top goals. Do you see any low-priority meetings that could have been declined? How about meetings that weren't particularly urgent?"

"Yes," said Iris as she scanned her calendar, "I accepted quite a few simply because I was available or because I felt obligated to a colleague or team." She pointed at a particular meeting. "I was asked to sit in on this presentation to a client—I barely said a word."

"It's hard to say no," I said. "But it's also hard to fall behind on projects and goals because you're trying to please everyone else."

Iris nodded. "I'm starting to see that I could contribute a lot more to Spex by turning down just a few low-priority, non-urgent meeting invitations each week."

"So refocusing on priorities could help you reclaim some time?"

"Absolutely," she said. "Okay, I'm starting to get the hang of the POSE tool, but," she frowned, "what about this?" Iris tapped the word *Objenda* on the POSE tool and said, "Ever heard of spell-check?"

O—What's the Objenda?

"The word *Objenda*," I replied with a hint of mock indignation, "is a fusion of the words *objective* and *agenda*."

"And why are you mashing two perfectly good words together?" asked Iris.

"Our research indicates that 90 percent of all professionals often attend meetings that lack a clearly stated objective and agenda.[2] The result is a meandering meeting that fails to achieve its purpose."

"Kind of like a rudderless ship," commented Iris.

"Exactly," I replied. "One big challenge is that most professionals think of the objective and agenda as *two* separate meeting elements."

"Aren't they?" asked Iris.

> ### *Hamster Tip*
> **A Great Objective:**
>
> - Is specific, action oriented, and measurable
>
> - Indicates when the outcome will be achieved
>
> - Reminds participants of the importance of the meeting
>
> - Is aligned with a well-crafted agenda
>
> *Weak objective*: To update team on sales progress and help each other sell more Spex media services.
>
> *Strong objective*: To develop five new team-selling tactics that will drive this year's sales over $5 million.

"No," I said firmly, "they're two parts of one thing. The objective is the destination for the meeting, and the agenda is the road map that plots the route required to reach the destination. Without both—"

"We get lost," said Iris thoughtfully. "So an Objenda is like a GPS. It explains exactly what a meeting hopes to achieve *and* the path to reaching that destination."

Iris looked at the POSE tool and frowned. "But how does that help me reduce meeting time?"

"Defining the Objenda will help you realize that a particular meeting might not be a top priority for you. For example, it might be a planning session, but you're only involved with the execution part of the project."

Iris took a sip of a vegetable drink she had brought on board. "So clarifying the Objenda helps us decline more unnecessary meetings?"

"Now you've got it," I said with a nod.

Iris frowned and pointed at herself. "But Coach, I—me, Iris—I rarely have an Objenda for my own meetings."

"You should," I encouraged. "It will infuse your meetings with purpose and help participants prepare. Clarifying the Objenda has one other big benefit. By fleshing out the objective and

> ### *Hamster Tip*
>
> #### A Great Agenda:
>
> - Describes a path to achieving the meeting's stated objective.
>
> - Answers the question: What will be covered by who and when?
>
> - Flexes to the situation. In other words, a quick 20-minute one-on-one meeting may only require two bullet-pointed agenda items in the meeting invitation.

agenda, you'll often realize when you don't have the *right people* attending."

Iris groaned, "I've sat through enough dead-end meetings to know that without the right people, decisions and actions are delayed."

"And that leads to more meetings," I replied.

"All right," said Iris. "From now on my motto is An Objenda for Every Meeting!"

She tapped the POSE tool insistently.

"What other questions can I POSE to save time?"

S—Can I Shorten Meeting Time?

"Are Grace and Erin ever late for class?" I asked.

"The kids are almost always on time," said Iris with a proud smile. She thought for a moment and then furrowed her brow. "So why are *grown-ups* always late for meetings?"

"Dominoes," I said.

"Huh?"

"Something truly remarkable happens every day in the business world. Millions of people wake up, go to work, and play a ridiculous game called Meeting Dominoes."

"What's that?" asked Iris.

"Meeting dominoes occur when back-to-back, 60-minute meetings are scheduled all through the day. This causes chaos because the first meeting ends right when the second one begins."

Iris was nodding. "We play *that* stupid game all the time. At school, the twins have a buffer between classes. So they have time to go to their locker, finish an assignment, or run to the bathroom—all the things people need to be productive and focused."

I nodded. "But in the business world we often set our meetings up without a buffer zone."

Iris shook her head. "Why do we do that?"

"There are several reasons. Organizations don't recognize how the frenzy between meetings erodes productivity. As a result, they never develop a strategy—"

"And the chaos continues," laughed Iris.

"Another big problem is that e-calendaring software is usually *preset* to either 30- or 60-minute meeting intervals. People tend to stick with the default settings."

Iris laughed and rolled her eyes. "It's true! I do it all the time. Because we're too lazy to override the standard meeting duration time, we run around like hamsters all day long."

"It does seem crazy," I agreed. "Iris, I'd like you to visualize something for me."

"Uh oh," she said. "Is this part of the initiation ritual?"

"No," I said with a smile, "that comes later. I'd like you to imagine the impact of Meeting Dominoes at Spex. Picture what happens over the course of a day for all of your colleagues."

Iris looked ahead and narrowed her eyes as if she were trying to see through the seat in front of her. "Yuck! I see 20 to 30 meetings convening at 9 a.m. all over Spex. At 10 a.m. everyone is scrambling to their second meeting—but they're already late."

"So the dominoes are falling?"

"Yes. Some are racing to their desks to jump on a teleconference that's already in progress. Many hit a technical snag that makes them even more stressed and late. Others, with face-to-face meetings, are dashing across the campus to another building."

"How do they feel?"

Iris laughed. "Stressed, cranky, and embarrassed. Some are trying to squeeze in an urgent phone call. Others are nervous that they're late for a meeting run by their boss or a key exec. They're out of breath, unprepared, and in desperate need of a bio-break."

"What about the people who are *on time?*"

"They're mad," she said, stealing a glance at her fellow passengers. "They resent the fact that so many people are habitually late."

Iris fell silent for a moment. She had a dazed look on her face.

"No wonder I'm a gigantic ball of stress," she said, turning to stare blankly out the window. "Meeting Dominoes has trapped me and everyone at Spex on the Hamster Wheel of Death!"

She turned toward me.

"How do we end this ridiculous game of dominoes?"

Hard 20/50s End Meeting Dominoes

I smiled. "With Hard 20/50s, which means:

- "Sticking with a clearly stated *hard* start and stop time for as many meetings as possible and

- "Scheduling 20- or 50-minute meetings instead of 30- or 60-minute meetings."

Iris frowned. "Look, Coach, just to be honest, this isn't the snazziest name you've come up with so far."

"I'm crushed," I said, pretending to be upset.

"But I like the idea of scheduling 20- and 50-minute meetings," she beamed. "Now I'll have 10 minutes to get to my next meeting and I'll be a lot more relaxed."

"And if you convert two or three 60-minute meetings to 50-minute meetings each day, then—"

"I'll save 20 to 30 minutes a day!" interrupted Iris with a satisfied look.

"Now," I said, "have you ever been in a meeting where someone says, *I've got a hard stop at a certain time?*"

"Sure," said Iris. "It creates a sense of urgency that keeps the meeting on track."

"From now on, you need to announce your hard stop at as many meetings as possible," I said.

"I'll do it," Iris agreed. Then she remembered something. "But what's a hard *start?*"

"It means that the meeting starts exactly when scheduled."

"That would be a radical change at Spex," joked Iris. "But seriously, how do I get everyone to do it?"

Five Minutes Early Is the New On Time

"Most people are late because they plan to be on time."

"Excuse me?" asked Iris with a frown.

"Planning to be on time is a bad idea because something unexpected—a traffic jam, a phone call, a technical glitch—often happens. If you're the meeting organizer, let everyone know that:

1. "The meeting will start exactly on time.

2. "Important information will be covered up front.

3. "A late start is not acceptable because the agenda is packed and members of the team have a hard stop at a certain time.

4. "They need to plan to arrive *five minutes early*. Ask them to build a buffer zone into their schedules to make it happen."

Iris was thinking. "So I have to make *five minutes early the new on time.*"

"That's brilliant," I said. "That's exactly what you need to do! You can even add *Arrive five minutes early* as a team ground rule and get the team to agree on a small penalty, like paying a small amount of money to a team charity, for being late."

Iris leaned forward. "Any other advice for my team? They can be stubborn."

"Here's a fun exercise that will get them to show up five minutes early."

Five Minutes Early Versus Five Minutes Late Exercise

"This exercise shows how being late hurts both productivity and professional image. Try this:

1. "Split the group into two sections.

2. "Have the first team come up with all the advantages of arriving five minutes early.

3. "Have the second team come up with all the disadvantages of arriving five minutes late.

4. "Discuss results and award a small prize for the group that comes up with the most answers.

"It's amazing to see how this exercise reminds people that careers are helped and hurt by the 10-minute difference between five minutes early and five minutes late. Want to try it?"

Iris and I took a moment to do the exercise. Kim and several passengers who had been listening intently to our conversation asked if they could join in.

Soon we had two groups of passengers competing to come up with the most answers. Kim offered free bags of airline pretzels to the winning team. In just a couple of minutes we had compiled the following two lists:

Five Minutes Early vs. Five Minutes Late Exercise	
Disadvantages to Being Late	**Advantages to Being Early**
1. Missing Objenda overview causes confusion	1. Time to review Objenda and own role
2. Looks unprofessional	2. Good for professional image
3. Lost opportunity to network	3. Networking opportunity
4. Stress about being late	4. Time to get a cup of coffee, relax
5. Meeting starts late and so ends late	5. Time to address urgent email or phone calls
6. Less time, so less productive meeting	6. Time to go to the bathroom
7. Boss mad	7. Boss happy
8. If you're not there, you can't contribute	8. Time for unexpected tech issues

After the exercise was completed (it was a tie, so everyone received pretzels), Iris took a moment to review her upcoming meetings.

"Take a look at this," she said, pointing at her e-calendar. "I've got eight back-to-back meetings in the next two weeks."

"Do you think you could contact the organizers and explain the concept of Hard 20/50s?"

Iris looked embarrassed. "Since I organized half of these meetings, I think I can guarantee at least a 50 percent success rate!"

I laughed and said, "Will you let me know what happens with the other half?"

"Sure," grinned Iris.

"Here are a few ways to reduce meeting time even more."

Mini-Meetings

"In many cases, a 5- or 10-minute meeting is all you need. Get in the habit of suggesting a mini-meeting. This is a 5- to 15-minute session that replaces the standard 30- to 60-minute meeting. A great way to ensure that live mini-meetings end on time is to agree to hold them standing up."

"*That* would create a sense of urgency," said Iris.

Leapfrog

I continued. "Have you ever noticed that many meetings and conversations end with a vague suggestion of a future meeting? For example, *Let's set up a teleconference after the holidays.*"

"Sure," said Iris.

"What typically happens when the time comes to hold these important follow-up meetings?"

Iris sighed. "We usually waste a lot of time trying to nail down a time and place that works for everyone."

"A better approach is to *leapfrog* those scheduling problems by quickly converting *suggested* meetings into *scheduled* ones," I said. "You do this by scheduling the next meeting at the end of the current one."

"Thus avoiding all the time-consuming hassles of scheduling later," observed Iris.

I nodded. "You save scheduling time and keep busy clients and VIPs engaged in your projects."

"We could use this frog idea," agreed Iris. "The most common excuse I hear from our sales reps is that they've asked a client for another meeting, but the client hasn't responded."

The Mini-Leapfrog

I smiled. "Have your people try this. Whenever I'm concluding a session with a client, I always leapfrog to the next presentation by saying, *Rather than waste our valuable time playing telephone or email tag, could we schedule a brief, 15-minute follow-up meeting right now?"*

"Hey!" said Iris in a moment of recognition, "you're combining the leapfrog and mini-meeting concepts. You're reminding the client that they'll save time by scheduling the next meeting now. And I'll bet they'll be much more open to a brief mini-meeting than our usual one-hour follow-up meeting. I think this would save time and increase client contact at Spex."

"Which would lead to what?" I asked with a smile.

"More sales," said Iris hopefully.

Shift to Virtual Meetings

"Another way to shorten meeting time is to increase the percentage of virtual meetings on your calendar."

Iris shook her head. "But we stink at virtual meetings."

I raised my hand. "So I'm going to show you how to make them much more effective."

"If that happens," said Iris, "and I'm not convinced it will, we could save a lot of time by reducing travel between meetings."

"We'll work on virtual meeting skills later," I promised. "But now let's cover the fourth and final question we need to POSE in order to cut unnecessary meeting time."

E—Am I E-vailable?

"A blend of electronic and available?" guessed Iris.

"Right," I said. "Our e-calendars often fail to reflect our true availability."

"Like when a top executive commits to attending an Operation Elevation meeting and then backs out?" asked Iris.

I nodded. "Exactly. Perhaps they had an opening on their calendar but actually had other invisible responsibilities that they failed to take into account. E-vailability means that you improve your e-calendaring skills so that your e-calendar reflects true availability."

Iris opened her e-calendar and we looked at her upcoming meetings.

Color Coding for E-Calendars

"I notice that you don't use color coding," I commented.

"I didn't know I could," replied Iris.

"You can, and it's a great way to prioritize meetings. Here's how I use colors within my calendar:

- "**Green** is for high-priority meetings with internal or external clients. A green traffic light symbolizes moving forward; it's the color of growth and—in some countries—money.

- "**Blue** is for meetings that revolve around the development of your primary offering or output. In my case it's coaching, books, and other things that I deliver to clients. Royal blue signifies quality in many parts of the world.

- "**Gold** is for team meetings. Our team is always striving to be the best."

"That's pretty corny," mocked Iris. "But at least it's easy to remember."

- "**Red** is for the time I've allocated for administrative activities like completing an expense report or doing email. Red reminds me to be a little cautious about spending too much time on administrative tasks versus high-ROI client activities.

- "**Purple** is for personal and family meetings or commitments. It's the color of royalty, which reminds me of the supreme importance of time spent with family and friends.

"With color coding[3] I can easily see concentrations of high- and low-priority meetings. It provides clues that help me realize that I'm not E-vailable at a particular time. For example, when I have three client meetings on Tuesday morning, I've found it wise not to schedule a great deal on Monday afternoon."

"Because you need time to prepare?" asked Iris.

"Absolutely," I replied. "In fact, I'll actually add the prep session to my e-calendar."

Schedule Me-Time

"You make an appointment with yourself?" asked Iris.

"I call it Me-Time," I said, "and I use it to signal to myself and others that I'm not E-vailable at that time. As a result I meet less and get important work done."

"I always get a splitting headache when I schedule too much on a single day," said Iris. "In fact, I had a teleconference right before the Operation Elevation meeting and I didn't leave enough time to prepare."

Return 3 & e

"Here's a final time-saving E-vailability tip: Return 3 & e. When you're trying to set up a meeting with a colleague or client, always provide them with a minimum of *three* available meeting times. Then ask them to e-schedule the time that works best."

"Wait a minute," said Iris. "What if it's a customer and I don't know if their e-calendar software is compatible with ours?"

"Why not ask them?" I offered. "It may provide you with a competitive advantage."

"How so?" asked Iris.

"With an e-invitation, a client only needs to hit Accept to agree to a meeting with you. That's easier than writing an email and then going through the hassle of having their assistant set up the meeting."

Iris nodded. "Return 3 & e could save us a lot of time on scheduling. It could also help us have more meetings with our clients, which will increase our sales. I'm going to use the POSE tool for the next few weeks and see if it saves me time."

I smiled. "All you have to do is POSE the—"

"Right questions," interrupted Iris.

- "Priority?
- "Objenda?
- "Shorten? and
- "E-vailable?"

"Wow," I said. "Your mind's like a steel trap."

"Thanks," said Iris with a smile, "but after a day jammed with meetings it feels more like a leaky bucket. What's next?"

Looking at my watch, I said, "Aren't we landing soon?"

"Oh, come on, Coach," pleaded Iris. "This hamster thing is just getting interesting. Let's get to it."

"Yeah, Coach," said the businessman across the aisle—the one who had gotten off on the wrong foot with Iris. "Cut the small talk and get to the next lesson. We've still got 20 minutes before we touch down!"

Your Hamster Revolution Assignment

Participants:

- Evaluate meeting invitations in relation to your goals.

- Try to eliminate two hours' worth of low-priority, optional meetings per week.

- When appropriate, ask the facilitator to clarify the meeting Objenda and request transition time if meetings are scheduled back to back.

Facilitators:

- Use Objendas and Hard 20/50s for every meeting.

- POSE the right questions so that you can eliminate two hours of low-priority meetings per week.

- Be open to suggestions from participants.

6

YOU'RE DRAFTED

"Okay, Iris, we've discussed a list of basic meeting elements that are missing at Spex meetings."

"A very long list," agreed Iris.

"Did you ever wonder *why* these ingredients are missing?"

"Well, things are so rushed these days. Who has the time to draft an Objenda or ground rules?" Iris reflected for a moment. "There are so many elements that contribute to a great meeting—how can anyone keep track of them all?"

I nodded. "What you need is a tool that *locks in* the right ingredients."

"And might you have such a tool for me?" asked Iris with a sly smile.

"As luck would have it, I do," I said as I pointed to the next tool on the Hamster Revolution job aid. "It's called a Meeting Power Draft, and we're going to build one right now."

I pointed to Iris' computer. "Please create a new email."

"Hold on," said Iris, raising her paw. "What does email have to do with…"

"Don't worry," I said with a smile. "It'll make sense in a minute."

Iris frowned as she created the email. "What now?"

"Let's make the subject of this email '0. Meeting Power Draft.'"

Iris looked a bit lost.

"Okay, it's titled."

"Now type four or five key elements of a well-run meeting on separate lines. Place a colon after each one."

Iris looked puzzled. "You mean like Objenda and Ground Rules? We should probably add Materials Needed and Logistics, too." She typed in the meeting elements and then said, "Now what?"

"Hit Save."

"Okay."

"Where is that email stored now?" I asked.

Iris thought for a minute. "When you save an email it goes to the Drafts folder." She checked her Drafts folder and sure enough, the new email was there. It looked like this:

Email
To:
Cc:
Subject: 0. Meeting Power Draft
Objective:
Agenda:
Materials Needed:
Logistics:
Ground Rules:

"Now here's the fun part," I said. "Click and drag that email into your calendar shortcut."

Iris did the maneuver.

"Hmmm. It becomes a calendar invitation."[4] Suddenly her eyes lit up. "Wait a minute, this is a meeting template that I can use over and over again. And look, the original Meeting Power Draft is still in my Drafts folder—it *doesn't* get deleted."

"Wasn't that easy?" I asked.

Something dawned on Iris. "Hey, Coach, I have different kinds of meetings that I run each month. Could I create customized Meeting Power Drafts for each one?"

"Yes. You might want to create one for your teleconferences."

Iris slapped my arm with her paw. "Right! That way I won't have to dig up my teleconference number and passcode for every meeting."

"You might want to title that '1. Teleconference Power Draft.'"

"Why do I need to add the 1?"

"So that you when you sort by subject in your Drafts folder, all your power drafts will rise neatly to the top."

Iris raised her eyebrows. "Smart. So they're easy to find."

She added her teleconference information to a third Meeting Power Draft and then decided to create a meeting invitation for an upcoming sales team meeting. She clicked and dragged the Meeting Power Draft into her e-calendar and filled in each field.

"This is a perfect reminder to create an Objenda," she said confidently.

Iris' new meeting invitation looked like this:

Meeting Power Draft

Subject: Spex Southwest Sales Team 3rd Quarter Planning Session
Location: Teleconference—See info below
Time: 10-10:50 a.m.

Objective:
Develop strategic plans for 10% sales increase for all 12 Southwest districts

Agenda:

1. Review YTD sales figures and strategies—Vijay Patel, 10 minutes

2. Review market trends and opportunities—Iris, 10 minutes

3. Establish 2 new strategies—Team, 30 minutes

Logistics:
Teleconference number: (123) 456-4321—Passcode: 534876

Preparation/Prework:
—Review sales plan, strategy, and results to date
—Share successful initiatives with team

"It looks great," I encouraged. "You can also create Meeting Power Drafts with some web conferencing programs."

"It's simple," she said enthusiastically. "It saves time and I don't have to think about what to include."

"And all of this is summarized on your Hamster Revolution for Meetings Power Tools card," I said.

"Good," said Iris, looking at the card I had given her earlier. "I see you've included a number of options."

"Right," I said. "This is a flexible tool. We wanted you to see all the possibilities. You don't have to use them all."

"Useful," nodded Iris.

Email

To:

Cc:

Subject: 0. Meeting Power Draft

Objective:
- Your meeting's destination or purpose

Agenda:
- Road map to reaching your objective

Action Items:
- Use 3-W's (Who-What-When)

Parking Lot Items:
- Off topic issues to be addressed later

Material Needed:
- Items needed by participants

Logistics:
- Web link, passwords, and bridge line

Ground Rules:
- Develop with your team

"Exactly," I smiled. "Now here's some final advice on Meeting Power Drafts:

- **"Limit ingredients**: At first it may be tempting to cram every imaginable ingredient into your Meeting Power Draft, but that makes the tool time-consuming to complete. Three or four ingredients are plenty.

- **"Mandatory Objenda**: Always make Objective and Agenda your first two fields.

- **"Remind recipients**: Use the Location field to tell recipients that a power draft can be found below in your meeting invitation. People are used to seeing an empty space in a typical e-calendar invitation."

Iris nodded. "It's funny that meeting invitations have standard fields for time and date but nothing for what actually happens *in* the meeting."

"It's strange," I agreed. "And here's another reason to use Power Drafts consistently: eventually every participant will know where to find the critical information for your meetings."

Iris' eyes brightened. She held up her PDA. "And all they'll have to do is check the e-calendar on their smart phone."

"After a couple weeks it will become second nature," I agreed. "And that means they'll be better prepared."

"You've got it, Iris. You're about to escape the meeting cage."

Kim announced that we would be landing soon. We shut down and stowed our laptops. The time had flown by and Iris was excited to learn more. As the plane landed we exchanged contact information and chatted about life, hobbies, and dreams.

"I'm a little wary," warned Iris as we walked down the jet bridge tunnel into the airport. "Give me a few days to try the

Hamster Revolution in the real world. If I see a big difference, I'll get approval for step three of the hamster plan, virtual meetings."

She paused outside the airline gate and turned to me—a tiny hamster dwarfed by busy passengers rushing by, trying to disguise their shock. Still, she had the strength and bearing of a gifted leader.

"I just want to warn you, our virtual meetings are a mess. If you can fix them..." Iris looked cautious. "Then maybe we can talk about making the Hamster Revolution a part of Operation Elevation. Though I'm not sure even a revolution could save this project."

"Whenever you're ready, challenge accepted," I said, bending down to shake her extended paw. "And we won't just save Operation Elevation; we'll make it a career milestone for you."

Iris nodded. "Well, right now it feels more like a career tombstone."

She turned and walked away from our gate looking far less frazzled than when we first met.

Your Hamster Revolution Assignment

Participants:

- If you attend a meeting that lacks key ingredients, show the leader how to use a Meeting Power Draft.

- Explain that it will help you and other participants to be more prepared.

Facilitators:

- Create a Meeting Power Draft and use it to plan an upcoming meeting.

- Be sure to explain to participants that key meeting information will now be embedded in the e-invitation.

7

IRIS CHECKS IN

To: The Info Coach
From: Iris
Subject: Great News! The Hamster Revolution for Meetings Works!

Hi, Coach,

I am excited to share some initial results with you:

1. I used the POSE tool to eliminate 4 unnecessary meetings coming up in the next 2 weeks. Time saved = 5 hours.

2. I also used Hard 20/50s to shave 10 minutes from 6 more appointments. Time saved = 1 hour. At this pace, I will save over 20 days a year!

3. I have already scheduled several meetings using Meeting Power Drafts, color coded my e-calendar, and set up plenty of Me-Time. All of these ideas are saving me time and helping me to get more done.

Important: Virtual Meeting Offer Accepted

I am eager to move forward with your virtual meeting evaluation offer. If it's okay with you, I won't use any of the hamster principles you taught me on the plane for these remote meetings. I want you to see what meetings are really like at Spex without the Hamster Revolution!

Thanks again,

Iris

To: Iris
From: The Info Coach
Confirmed: I can make all three of the virtual meeting dates you sent

---

Hi, Iris—Congrats on your hamster success!

Confirmed: I can attend all of the virtual meetings you suggested.

Background:

- I think it's a great idea to hold off on applying hamster principles to these meetings. My goal is to evaluate your team's exact needs and provide tailored solutions.
- I will be observing but not otherwise participating in the meetings.

Next steps: After the meetings I'll provide you with feedback and tools.

Great work so far, Iris!

The Info Coach
info@infoexcellence.com

1-888-340-3598
www.infoexcellence.com

8

VIRTUAL MEETING MAGIC

Over the next few days I attended two of Iris' virtual meetings, and just as she'd said, they were awful. In our follow-up phone call I reviewed my notes with her:

Meeting 1: Regional Sales Managers' Weekly Teleconference

Notes: *Iris led a somewhat dry teleconference that was designed to summarize key initiatives for the week. She was the primary speaker for 90 percent of the meeting, and when she asked questions, there was usually a long silence before anyone responded. Most of the conversation from other participants came from 3 of her 12 regional managers. Other team members seemed bored and distant, as if they were doing email.*

Meeting 2: Brainstorming Teleconference with Marketing

Notes: *Iris attended a brainstorming session led by Tasha Williams from marketing. Iris gave her input on a variety of ideas, and the meeting was lively but unproductive. Unfortunately, the group was unable to come to a conclusion on a specific theme for an important new campaign. They agreed to hold another teleconference in a few weeks.*

After sharing my notes, I asked Iris if she agreed with my assessment.

"Yes," she said glumly. "These meetings could put coffee to sleep. When you can't see people, shake their hand, or interact with them, it's impossible to hold their attention."

✓ Upgrade from Phone to Web

"Okay," I said, "let's solve this focus problem. Here's a quick question: Both of the virtual meetings I attended were teleconferences. What do you have against web conferences?"

"The weekly sales managers' meeting has always been a teleconference," protested Iris, "and sometimes team members are traveling and can't be on their computers."

"I understand," I said. "But most of them can be at their computers—right?"

"Yeees," agreed Iris, with a hint of trepidation.

"My point is that switching to web conference opens up a ton of options to make your meeting more dynamic and interactive. Here are three reasons to make the switch:

1. "Adding a visual element instantly increases engagement. In fact, research shows that graphics increase comprehension by 50 percent.[5]

2. "Web conferences have many features like surveys and chat that can boost interactivity.

3. "It's harder to ignore a meeting and do email if something visual, interactive, and interesting is happening on your computer."

"Good reasons," mused Iris. "Maybe I'll try to hold a few more web conferences next month."

"No," I countered, "I'd like you to begin the phone to web upgrade right now. After all, this is a telephone meeting—why not turn it into a web conference?"

"Is that really necessary?"

"Yes," I said emphatically. "Would you ever hold a live meeting in a pitch black room?"

"Of course not," said Iris.

"In many ways a teleconference is like meeting in the dark. When we add visuals via web conference we turn the lights on and activate our meetings."

"Activate?"

"People are crazy-busy, Iris. Graphs, websites, polls, and video can energize, engage, and persuade your audience."

"Persuasion is good," said Iris. She was obviously thinking of Spex' clients.

"But upgrading *planned* meetings isn't enough," I insisted. "There are times when *instantly* upgrading a random phone call to a web meeting can really help you get your point across."

I quickly directed Iris to a web conferencing website and gave her a passcode. In seconds she was staring at a chart on my computer screen.

"Imagine trying to describe this chart verbally," I said.

"I see the chart...and your point," quipped Iris.

"This chart will help you select the right virtual meeting format," I said.

The Hamster Revolution		
Choose the Right Meeting Format Chart		
Meeting Format	**Pros**	**Cons**
Live Meetings	Best for sensitive, controversial, and complex topics, richest form of communication exchange, allows for strong interaction before and after meeting.	Most expensive format, requires much more transition time, high travel/ building costs, increases carbon footprint.
Teleconference	Easy to set up and few technology issues, reduces carbon footprint, reduces travel/building costs.	No visuals, many distractions, less opportunity for interaction = lost focus, hard to interject opinion with large group, people tune out and do email.
Web Conference	Highly interactive, visual cues increase comprehension, many interactivity tools, easy to gain instant feedback, reduces carbon footprint, lowers travel/building costs, can include low-resolution participant video image.	Technical glitches common, more effort to set up, most employees not familiar with advanced features, participant video can be low quality.
Videoconference	Allows for seeing participants' nonverbal expressions, which can sometimes be extremely important; somewhat interactive; reduces carbon footprint; reduces travel costs; higher-end systems from HP, Cisco, and others are breaking new ground in telepresence, which is the sensation that people are in the same room; Hi Def picture is crystal clear.	Visual action not always exciting or engaging, less interactive, more technical problems, can be expensive, embarrassing if colleague is wearing pajamas.

New Meeting Alternatives

Meeting Format	Pros	Cons
Wikis	Participants do not have to meet at the same time, built-in storage of information and commentary, reduces travel and meeting time, reduces carbon footprint, reduces travel costs.	Limited dialogue, some may not contribute or even participate, another website to keep track of, technology new to some employees, many lose passwords or URL.
Blogs	Participants do not have to meet at the same time, allows for discussion and input from entire team, reduces travel and meeting time, lowers carbon footprint, reduces travel costs.	Can be a time drain, some may not return to see colleague comments, may not result in completion of tasks, must be tracked and summarized by someone, technology new to some employees, many lose passwords or URL.
Instant Messaging	Excellent for mini-meetings or arranging quick phone calls, some allow for file transfer and whiteboard features, great way to reach experts fast.	Not as good for groups, increases interruptions, limited nonverbal cues, can devolve into low-priority chat/time waster.
Social Networking	Sites like Facebook and LinkedIn create communities of like-minded people, experts can share info without formal meetings, other examples include My Space, Plaxo, and Twitter. Even Google, Live Search, and Wikipedia represent low-cost ways to interact with other experts without having to meet with them. All approaches save time and reduce carbon footprint.	Info may be too general, experts are not accountable for opinions or accuracy of info, misinformation and disinformation campaigns increasingly common, social networking sites and RSS feeds generate more email and interruptions, info must be carefully filtered for relevance and accuracy, search based more on popularity than veracity.

After reviewing the chart Iris said, "This is good information and it really does help to see it instead of just hearing you talk about it. I don't see why I couldn't hold more web meetings."

"Switching from phone to web is your *biggest* opportunity to hold more productive virtual meetings," I said emphatically.

Iris frowned. "Well, maybe we should go one step further and jump to videoconferencing. Then we could actually see each other talking."

Videoconferencing

"Videoconferencing is amazing technology," I said. "At times, the ability to see everyone is crucial, but that isn't always the case."

"Why not?"

"We're used to seeing well-produced, action-packed, high-definition video on the Internet and TV. By contrast, staring at people in a static conference room for two hours can be a bit dull. What does that visual image really add?

"By contrast, web conferencing puts the focus on the business at hand by highlighting the presentation, document, or website being discussed. While videoconferencing is advancing and has many uses, particularly for high-end executive meetings, I recommend honing your basic web meeting skills first."

"Now that you mention it," said Iris, "Operation Elevation people will be working from home where they'll dress more casually."

"So they may not appreciate suddenly being on camera?" I asked.

"I know a few coworkers who can't wait to commute across the hallway in their boxer shorts," chuckled Iris. After a brief laugh she asked a serious question. "Why have you included wikis and blogs in your chart? I don't consider those to be meetings."

Wikis

"Not in the traditional sense," I agreed. "But a wiki, which saves time by allowing visitors to add, delete, and edit relevant information on a series of web pages, has many characteristics of a traditional meeting. People convene in one place, share ideas, argue, and record insights. It's a form of collaboration."

"How does that save time?" asked Iris, still sounding skeptical.

"Wikis can eliminate the need for weekly update meetings while also providing an excellent way to store ideas and best practices."

Iris sounded confused. "Can you give me an example?"

"Sure," I said. "Our research team used to hold a weekly meeting to share new info with our sales and marketing team. Our salespeople began to complain that they didn't have time for the meeting. To make matters worse, it was hard to keep track of all the data because it was constantly being updated."

"Uh oh," said Iris. "We've got the same issue with our market research group."

"So we developed an internal wiki that allowed our research team to publish Hamster Revolution research papers, facts, and insights to an editable series of web pages."

"That could save time," mused Iris. "But how can blogs replace meetings?"

Blogs

"We use internal blogs to gain input from busy colleagues. They can surf to a blog and provide feedback on a new ad campaign or corporate policy without having to gather for a meeting."

"And they don't need to convene a series of meetings," said Iris thoughtfully, "which saves time."

Instant Messaging

"Exactly," I said. "And instant messaging is another great way to avoid a more formal one-on-one meeting or phone call. Since 72 percent of phone calls are answered by machines,[6] instant messaging allows me to meet briefly with a colleague, ask them a small number of important questions, and then get back to work. I recommend establishing the IM1B rule at Spex: Limit **I**nstant **M**essages to **1** Minute for **B**usiness only."

"IM could drive interruptions through the roof," noted Iris. "Spex has these tools but we haven't discussed the best way to use them."

She paused and then said, "But I have to be honest, my biggest problem is that ever since we started holding more virtual meetings, I've had this sinking feeling that no one is listening and things aren't getting done."

"Here's the big secret," I said quietly. "Going virtual can actually make your meetings *more* exciting, interactive, and effective."

Iris sounded unsure. "How can you get people *more* involved when they're not in the room?"

Five Alive

"You adopt a Hamster Revolution strategy called *Five Alive*," I said, revealing a checklist document via our web conference.

The Hamster Revolution for Virtual Meetings

Five Alive Activation Checklist™

Passive Attendees	Active Participants
☐ Upgrade phone meetings to web meetings	
☐ Call on everyone – quiet ones first	
☐ Try spontaneous, anonymous phone surveys	
☐ Be a virtual chat champion	
☐ Master web conference surveys	
☐ Use virtual meeting icebreakers	
☐ Take a trip around the world	
☐ Replace brainstorming with Brainsurfing	
☐ Toss it!	
☐ Make better use of pictures and intros	

Meetings have changed! The virtual shift is on!

"Five Alive means that you plan a variety of interactive events every 5 to 10 minutes in order to activate and engage your audience."

There was a long pause and I heard Iris give a frustrated sigh. "How in the world would I be able to do that? In a live meeting I can move about the room, call on different people, or walk close to someone who is falling asleep or doing email instead of paying attention. I can use hand gestures to make a point or write on flip chart…but all of that is completely wiped out in the virtual world."

"I understand," I said. "But you also gain some dynamic new ways to reach out to participants."

"You're going to have to connect the dots for me," said Iris flatly.

"Okay," I said. "In addition to upgrading from phone to web, here are nine more ways to keep your audience on the edge of their virtual seats."

✓ Call on Everyone—Quiet Ones First

It's wise to review a list of meeting participants before the virtual meeting. As people join the phone portion of the meeting, I like to say, *Hi. Who just joined us? How's the weather there? Aren't you glad it's Friday?* This allows you to build rapport and sets the expectation that everyone is going to be involved with the meeting."

"I guess it makes sense to interact quickly—before everyone tunes out," said Iris. "This just might work with Alex."

I continued, "I also share that this is going to be a very interactive session and that I will be calling on everyone to be sure we do our best collective thinking. You should try to interact with each person at least once during the course of the meeting. Finally, give some thought as to who the quietest participants will be and develop a plan to call on them early in the meeting. For example, have less talkative participants do low-risk interactions like review action items from your last meeting. Great questions include:

- *"Hey, Sanjay, this is your area of expertise—what do you think?*
- *"Maria, your team was above quota and within budget—tell us how you did it.*

"Once a quiet person is engaged, it's much easier to gain further input as the meeting progresses."

"This is really helpful," said Iris. "Keep going!"

✓ Try Spontaneous, Anonymous Phone Tone Surveys

"Okay. An easy way to get the attention of meeting participants is to conduct an anonymous phone tone survey. Pose a provocative question and ask everyone to hit the 9 key on their phone pad if they agree. Phone tone surveys are great for short, simple questions like:

- *"Is anyone confused by what I just shared?*
- *"Have you learned something that will save you time?"*

Iris hit a button on her keypad. *Beep.* "Hey, that's fast and easy. I also like the fact that it's anonymous—I could get some good instant feedback from my team and keep them involved."

"Here's another idea that will help you create a dynamic, interactive session," I said.

✓ Be a Virtual Chat Champion

"Can you see the chat box on the right-hand side of the screen of this web meeting?" I asked.

"Sure," said Iris.

"I'd like you to start using chat more in your virtual meetings. First, tell your participants that you want them to be active meeting participants by posting any comment they like during the meeting."

"Whoa!" said Iris, sounding shocked. "Anything? At any time?"

"Yes."

"I disagree," said Iris defiantly. "It would be very distracting if people commented and joked all the way through one of my virtual presentations."

"That's what I thought, too," I said. "But one of my clients insisted that I leave the chat box open during an important presentation. People made jokes and even challenged some of what I said, but I quickly realized that the banter was *riveting* people to the web conference."

"They were riveted?" asked Iris, sounding incredulous and perhaps a bit envious.

"Instantly," I said. "And I found that I could weave participant comments and objections right into the presentation. As it turned out, the jokes added a lot of fun to the presentation. I also knew when I lost or confused my audience."

"How?" asked Iris.

"Because they would mention it in the chat. They would type *Huh?* or *Can you go over that again?* It's much easier to ask for clarification via chat than by verbally interrupting a speaker."

"Because the speaker doesn't need to stop while others comment," reasoned Iris.

"I've also discovered that some of the quietest people on my team are the best at expressing themselves via chat. When they express an opinion through chat, you can ask them a follow-up question, and suddenly you have a brand new voice contributing to your meeting. You can also use chat as an informal survey tool."

Iris began thinking out loud. "There's a deathly silence whenever I ask for feedback in a teleconference. Everyone waits for someone else to speak up. It also takes them a moment to unmute their phones. It's awkward. But a chat survey would be quick and easy."

"Extremely easy," I agreed.

"I see," said Iris. "It draws people in and no one gets drowned out."

"Right," I replied. "Some web conferencing programs even provide a printed record of the chat, which can be useful in following up after the meeting. Here are a few more ways to become a virtual meeting chat champion:

- "Have a team member present a challenge they are experiencing and ask all participants to type possible answers in the chat box. In many cases this can lead to innovative new approaches for the entire team.

- "Ask all participants to share their biggest success or challenge of the week. This will instantly bring people closer together as they see their colleagues' triumphs and struggles flash in front of them."

"I bet you gather some powerful team-building info that way," mused Iris.

"True," I replied. "I also love getting quick feedback on the meeting itself via chat."

"Can you give me an example?"

"Sure." I typed *Please type one word into the chat box that best describes this meeting.*

Iris typed *Gruesome.* We both chuckled.

I typed *But improving!*

"Hey, that's not one word," joked Iris, adding, "Okay. I'll make chat a big part of our new Five Alive strategy. What's next?"

✓ Master Web Conference Surveys

"This," I said, launching a survey question on our web conferencing tool:

In this meeting, I've discovered at least five new virtual meeting tips that will boost my productivity. (True or False)

"Fun," laughed Iris, as she clicked on the True button. I clicked on a button that shared the results of my very small poll with her.

"Does your web conference software have a survey tool?" I asked.

"Yes," said Iris. "You can launch a question and it instantly creates a bar chart."

"Do you know how to use it?" I asked.

"Not really," said Iris, sounding a bit embarrassed. "In fact, I've only seen it used once or twice in the past five years at Spex."

"I hear that a lot," I said. "It's an underutilized tool. Web conference surveys gather great data, provide instant feedback, and glue your participants to their computer screens."

"I guess it's hard to do email when you're voting in a survey," laughed Iris.

"You can ask funny and serious questions," I said. "You can find out if a team strategy is working or not."

Iris sighed into the phone. "And people are more invested when they feel that their opinion matters. I'll figure out how our survey tool works and give it a try."

✓ Use Virtual Meeting Icebreakers

"On a personal note," I asked, "did you learn anything new about your team in this week's sales teleconference?"

"Not a thing, Coach," said Iris after a long pause.

"Did anything happen that would make your people feel closer as a team?"

"Nope," she said, with a hint of resignation in her voice. "And it seems like we're drifting apart as things have gotten more and more virtual. We used to hold a live regional managers' meeting six times a year. Now that only happens twice."

"Why not try a virtual meeting icebreaker to shrink the distance between members of your team?"

"I don't know, Coach. We're very busy and these meetings are packed with information."

"Then again," I countered, "what good is covering a lot of information if participants aren't paying attention or don't feel connected to the project or team?"

"I see your point, but I'm still pretty sure that we could never budget 15 minutes for a team-building exercise," protested Iris.

"A Hamster Revolution Five Alive icebreaker helps bring your team together in *two or three* minutes."

"How does it work?" asked Iris.

"Prior to your meeting, you send an email to your people and ask them to privately answer a few fun questions: What is your favorite movie, contemporary book, TV show, vacation site, or restaurant. Pop the answers into a spreadsheet and then at the beginning of next week's web conference, turn the answers into a question:

"Can anyone guess the identity of this team member?

- "Favorite movie: *Gone with the Wind*
- "Favorite business book: *The One Minute Manager*
- "Best trip ever: Fantasy Baseball camp"

"I get it," said Iris. "It's a quick way to get to know each other and build team spirit. I could also ask them for a favorite sports team, a baby picture, a pet peeve—the possibilities are endless."

"And just one quick email can provide you with dozens of icebreaker quizzes that can be used over the next few months. It's fast, fun, and effective. Now buckle your seat belt, because we're going on a trip around the world!"

"Excuse me?" laughed Iris. "I *know* that's not in the budget!"

✓ Take a Trip Around the World

"Actually, this trip is free," I said, switching the web conference to a view of my computer screen and an open web browser.

"The web can take us anywhere in a flash, which is far more interesting than watching a static slide presentation. For example, Internet mapping software can give you a satellite view of any building, mountain, body of water, or sports arena in the world."

"Yeah," said Iris cautiously, "but that sounds as if we'd only be joyriding around the net without getting much done."

"Really?" I asked, navigating to a satellite view of Mount Everest. "Wouldn't this be a more powerful way to visually convey the meaning of Operation Elevation?"

"It might," admitted Iris. "Everyone would pay attention to that."

I continued, "In your weekly sales manager teleconference you instructed your team to study a competitor that had been cutting into your sales."

"We've been losing business to SBQ," said Iris, "but we didn't have time—"

She paused as I brought up the SBQ website and instantly framed a number of client testimonials, product descriptions, and account executive profiles.

"Hey!" cried Iris. "That's Gina Schaeffer. She used to work for us! Maybe that's how they're getting into all of our accounts."

There was a long pause on the phone. "Iris? Are you there?"

"I'm sorry," said Iris, sounding guilty, "I got a little distracted by the SBQ website—I'm jotting down some notes—it sparked some ideas."

"Can you see how taking a trip around the world can make your virtual meetings more productive?" I asked.

"I guess there *are* some things that are easier to do in a virtual meeting," said Iris. "It's actually quite fun to surf the Internet with another person. It's something we usually do alone."

"I'm glad I could keep you company," I said. "Here are some other web destinations to consider:

- "Websites that highlight respected research that validates a key point you're trying to make,

- "A blog that documents a hot new trend in your industry,

- "A media story highlighting a client need, organization success, or team member accomplishment,

- "A client site that shows who they are and what they hope to accomplish this year,

- "A motivational video that inspires your team,

- "A website that highlights the positive attributes of a team member's region, state, or town,

- "The website of a charity supported by a member of your team,

- "A sports website that highlights a friendly rivalry between two or more team members."

"Awesome," said Iris. "What's next?"

"I'd like to discuss your brainstorming session," I said.

"It wasn't exactly a storm of ideas," joked Iris. "The only thing we determined was the date for our next meeting."

✓ Replace Brainstorming with Brainsurfing™

"Let me guess," laughed Iris. "Our brainstorming session should've been a web conference. Right?"

"You're catching on," I said. "And I would try *Brainsurfing* instead."

"Danger!" said Iris, making a robotic beeping noise over the phone, "New hamster word alert! New hamster word alert!"

I was really beginning to enjoy her irreverent sense of humor.

"Brainstorming," I continued, "is tough in a live setting but even more difficult via teleconference. So—"

"We've got the whole world on the web," interrupted Iris.

"Right," I agreed. "Remember how you were trying to get the marketing team to visualize your idea about an Olympic sprinter running up the side of a high-rise building?"

"Sure," said Iris. "I just couldn't get them to understand."

"Next time, I want you to Brainsurf with them," I said as I opened a popular search engine and typed in *Olympic sprinter.*

"One rule for Brainsurfing with colleagues is to adjust your search engine preferences to filter out inappropriate web content," I said.

"Smart," said Iris. "There are definitely some things on the web that we *don't* need to see."

I clicked on the search engine's Images tab and suddenly the screen was filled with hundreds of runner photos and drawings.

"Oh!" said Iris as she scanned the images for a moment.

"See anything that resembles your vision?" I asked.

"Wait! That's the one right there—on the bottom left corner of the screen," shouted Iris. I narrowed the browser window so that it isolated a black-and-white graphic of a sprinter taking off. Then I launched a second browser window and we sifted through several hundred building images. We recorded the URLs for the photos that best matched Iris' vision. I rotated the best choice so the runner was going straight up.

"Since we don't own these pictures, we can't copy them," I said. "But there are some royalty-free picture sites that you *can* use." I surfed to one of my favorite royalty-free sites[7] and we downloaded several pictures that matched Iris' vision. I pasted the pictures into a Word document and played with the size and positioning for a moment.

"That's exactly how I pictured it," said Iris after a minute.

"Not quite," I said. "Why not use web conference drawing tools to show marketing where the text should go?"

"Drawing tools?" asked Iris. I took a moment to show Iris that most web conferencing programs allow participants to write, type, draw, and highlight right on their screens. Iris quickly got the hang of the tools. She added text suggestions, highlighted key elements of her photos, and even crossed out things that would need to be changed.

"You can even use a whiteboard to draw and sketch ideas in a virtual Brainsurfing meeting," I said.

I launched a virtual whiteboard and Iris further sketched her idea, which, by the way, I really liked. As she sketched a man running up the side of a building, I would periodically add a comment or two.

For good measure we surfed to Iris' top five competitors' sites to see if any of their marketing imagery overlapped with her vision. None did.

"We can even Brainsurf to ensure that we've created something that's both effective *and* original," said Iris, sounding pleased.

"It's also a great way to quickly check slogans, descriptions, and names that you create," I added.

"Amazing," crowed Iris. "I just emailed a screenshot of the final picture to Tasha in marketing. I hope she likes it!"

"Hey," I said, sounding hurt, "you're not supposed to be sending email during this meeting!"

"I'll never do it again," laughed Iris. "Any more participation tips?"

✓ Toss it!

"Yes. Don't be afraid to toss it!"

"We're not talking about cookies are we?" chided Iris.

"I'm talking about the web presentation itself," I said. "If someone on the web conference has an interesting document or presentation they're trying to describe, see if your web conferencing software allows you to instantly shift the presentation view to their computer."

"Then everyone can see what they're describing," reasoned Iris.

"Exactly, and your meeting suddenly gets more interesting and productive. It also makes the demonstrator feel smart and valued."

"Which makes it harder for them to tune out of the meeting," she observed.

"A lot harder," I said. "Another alternative is to transfer control of *your* computer to another team member. This can be handy when someone is trying to quickly show the team a tech tip or troubleshoot a software issue that exists only on their own laptop."

✓ Make Better Use of Pictures and Intros

"Let's end at the beginning," I said. "Do you include a picture of yourself when doing a web presentation for clients or Spex colleagues that aren't on your immediate team?"

"No," said Iris. "Should I?"

"There's a lot of truth to the old cliché *A picture's worth a thousand words.* So why wouldn't you include a professional-looking head shot that says great things about you?"

Iris mused, "Otherwise...I guess we're just voices and a slide show."

"A sharp-looking business head shot helps you look professional, friendly, and trustworthy. It can create a human connection between you and someone sitting 3,000 miles away."

"It could also make teammates feel a whole lot closer," added Iris thoughtfully.

"So you'll place a photo on your opening slide?" I asked.

"Okay," said Iris.

"I've noticed something else," I said, pressing on. "Most web presentations lack a really sharp introduction of the key speaker. Have you ever introduced Carl to a group of Spex executives or clients on a web conference?"

"Sure," said Iris.

"How do you do it?"

"I usually say, *And here's Carl,*" said Iris sheepishly.

I brought up a web video of Carl making an appearance on a local business television show.

"What if you worked out a really impressive 30-second intro and showed this in the background?" I asked.

"I think Carl might be embarrassed," said Iris flatly. "He's a humble guy."

"Perhaps," I conceded. "But prospective clients and busy execs want to know *why* they should invest the time to listen. You see, Iris, the *focus line* has moved."

"What ?" asked Iris.

"It means that people are living in a time-crunched world overloaded by information and interruptions. Their ability to focus is at an all-time low. If you fail to grab them in the first 15 seconds, then—"

"They vaporize," interrupted Iris.

"Excuse me?"

"We've noticed that half our clients disappear about five minutes into our webinars. It's been getting worse."

"Then you're losing an important information age battle," I said. "The battle for focus. A shining intro of Carl, great visuals, great content, and constant interaction will keep people involved and feeling valued."

"Lately, we've been losing the focus battle *and* the sales war," said Iris. "Just a minute." I could hear Iris talking to someone who had popped into her office.

"Uh oh, I have to run, Coach. David just poked his head in to tell me that the CEO needs an Operation Elevation update at 1:30. That's in 10 minutes. Yikes."

"Great," I said, "but I was hoping to discuss technology challenges—"

"No time today, Coach," said Iris firmly. "How about this? I'll share this High Five stuff with our team and—"

"That's Five Alive," I corrected.

"Right," said Iris, sounding distracted, "then I'll have David send you the invitation to our next client sales webinar on Friday. I'll bet we can make it twice as engaging with Five Alive. Sorry, but I've got to go."

"Sounds like a plan," I said. "Take care, Iris."

9

A SLOW-MOTION TRAIN WRECK

On Friday, I logged in to the Spex client sales webinar 15 minutes early hoping to see the sales team working like a well-oiled machine. What I witnessed was a slow-motion train wreck that probably hurt sales more than it helped.

I was the first arrival on both the teleconference and web meeting. Moments before start time, Carl opened the phone line and started the webinar. Immediately, I knew something was wrong. His voice sounded fuzzy and I detected an odd echo every time he spoke. The echo was so distracting that Carl must have known he couldn't proceed with the meeting. He muttered something about technical difficulties and then muted his phone.

One minute before start time, Iris and roughly 25 clients began to call in to the teleconference and log in to the web meeting. Most clients were a few minutes late. Very few were early.

"Hello—Hello—Hello?" they echoed to each other. Some laughed but others seemed perturbed.

"Am I in the right place?" asked a client.

"I don't have time for this," opined another.

I would later learn that some of them also had problems connecting to the web meeting. But Carl's biggest challenge was the echo chamber inside his teleconference.

At roughly five minutes past start time, Carl used the chat function to indicate that he had found a second teleconference line and that everyone should switch over to the new line.

As we all jumped to the new line we were relieved to hear that the echo was gone. Unfortunately, Carl still sounded fuzzy, and I realized that he was on his cell phone. Carl launched into his presentation sounding a bit stressed and rushed.

At about the 20-minute mark, once again, disaster struck. Carl's screen froze. It was the last straw for the normally mild-mannered Carl. His tone went from stressed to angry. He knew that all of these glitches were reflecting poorly on him and Spex.

He tried somewhat unsuccessfully to keep the banter going while he shut down and restarted his computer. This took about five more minutes. Iris introduced herself and mentioned a few things about Spex while Carl finally reentered the meeting.

A client suggested that Carl simply email the presentation to everyone. Carl tried this, only to find that the 15-megabyte presentation was rejected by a number of clients' email systems that had strict size limits for incoming messages.

The number of clients in the web meeting dwindled from 30 to 17 to 9.

With just 20 minutes to go, Carl finally resumed his online presentation. I could see that he had jettisoned all hope of using Five Alive techniques. There was no way he was going to risk launching an interactive survey question or surf to an interesting website now. He sounded beaten as he plodded through his slides in monotone.

As he continued to talk, I noticed that his voice was dropping out every now and then. I realized that the gaps were caused by the call-waiting feature on his cell phone. These gaps were incredibly distracting and I imagined that some of the calls were from clients trying to participate in the program. Carl attempted to ignore the call-waiting tones, which must have sounded like annoying beeps on his end. He stumbled on his words every few seconds.

Then the meeting delivered its final knock-out blow. One of Carl's well-meaning peers, a regional manager from across the country, decided to send him an instant message. The private message popped up on Carl's screen in full view of all participants. You could hear people gasp as they read it.

Instant Message:

Bob Gordon: *Carl! It's %$^#&$ screwed up! Your voice keeps dropping out and it sounds like $*%#^)*! Switch phones and speak up buddy!*

Carl sighed loudly and quickly closed the instant message. He concluded the meeting with a weak plea for clients to contact their Spex representative for more information.

I looked at my watch. *I wonder when I'll hear from Iris*, I thought.

Twenty-nine seconds later, my phone rang.

10

BECOMING A VIRTUAL
MEETING VIRTUOSO

It was Iris and Carl and they wanted answers.

"Okay, Coach," said Iris tensely, "how can we make sure this *never*, *ever* happens again?"

"Yeah," said Carl, who still sounded a bit shell-shocked. "Talk about Murphy's Law. Anything that could go wrong did go wrong!"

"Iris and Carl," I said calmly, "I have a new law for you. The Hamster Virtual Meeting Law: Everything will fail."

"That's real snappy," said Iris, sounding more than a bit irritated.

"And upbeat," noted Carl sarcastically. "You must be a hoot at parties. Seriously though, there was nothing I could've done to prevent all those technical problems."

"Oh, no?" I asked. "If you had expected things to go wrong you probably would have taken corrective steps. The law is rooted in the idea that virtual meetings have a ton of variables: your computer, your participant's computer, the phone line, the web line, and on and on."

I heard Carl exhale loudly and then there was a brief silence.

"We need an explanation," said Iris. "How can you stop a computer screen from freezing or a web conference line from echoing?"

"You need two things: 1) A way to *prevent* virtual meeting disasters, and 2) a plan that limits the damage caused by unexpected meeting glitches."

"Prevention and damage control," mused Iris. "Okay, we're listening."

"Don't just listen—I want you to see this." I had Carl and Iris log in to a web conference site and then I opened a new virtual meeting checklist.

"What does *semper paratus* mean?" asked Iris as she scanned the bottom of the tool.

"It's Latin for *always prepared*," I said, "and that's what you're going to be after you start using this checklist. I want to emphasize that many of these insights are for both leaders and participants. I also want to acknowledge that for a casual, one-on-one web meeting with a peer, this may be overkill. But for important web meetings with key associates or clients, this checklist will help you avoid a mountain of grief."

The Hamster Revolution	
Virtual Meeting Tech Glitch Checklist	
Prevent Problems	**Control Damage**
☐ Reboot computer before web meetings	☐ Back up presentation (PDF), teleconference, presenter
☐ Use the best possible phone/web connection	☐ Have teleconference and help center on speed dial
☐ Arrive early: use the 30/15 Rule	☐ Create technical difficulties slide
☐ Disable distractions: computer dings, pop-ups, phones, etc.	☐ Determine secondary communication plan
☐ Perform a sound, mute, and slide check	☐ Have a disaster recovery plan
☐ Practice web maneuvers	☐ Smile and remain positive

Bonus Strategy: Create and use a virtual meeting cheat sheet
The Hamster Virtual Meeting Law: Everything Will Fail!
Semper Paratus

"And a sea of humiliation," moaned Carl.

"I'm picturing Carl curled up in fetal position by his computer," laughed Iris.

"Don't worry, Carl," I said. "Help is on the way. Let's start by preventing technical glitches with a little preparation."

Virtual Meeting Tech Glitch Prevention Checklist

✓ **"Reboot your computer before web meetings**. Rebooting your computer clears short-term memory, which can reduce your chances of an embarrassing mid-session screen freeze. And to minimize glitches, it's always a good idea to keep as few programs open as possible."

"When Carl's screen froze on the sales webinar, I wanted to die!" said Iris. "We'd spent two months rounding up those clients, and we ended up looking like clowns."

"It was painful to watch," I agreed.

"And after I rebooted, at least my computer ran fine," noted Carl reluctantly.

"It did," I agreed. "So do it *before* every important web meeting. Another way to look your best is to make sure you're sending a clear signal. Here are some suggestions:"

✓ **"Use the best possible phone and web connection.**
I recommend using a hard phone line rather than a cell phone whenever possible. Cell phone quality varies, and this results in intermittent static, poor sound quality, and disconnections. Cell phone broadband and hotel wireless signals can also fluctuate with the number of users and the weather conditions. That could be another reason why Carl's screen froze. If you're traveling and need to attend an important meeting, you may want to try to locate a facility that offers a more reliable connection.

✓ **"Arrive early: use the 30/15 Rule.** If you're hosting an *important* web conference, try to log in 30 minutes early to test the web and phone connection. If possible, have a colleague join you and make sure that all the log-in information and interactive tools you plan to use are working fine."[8]

"It seems a bit extreme to log in 30 minutes early," said Iris.

"In most cases the pre-check only takes five minutes," I said, "and you can do productive work while waiting for others to join the meeting. But when things go wrong—as they did today—you often need 10 to 20 minutes to isolate the problem, reboot your computer, contact the help center, and figure out an alternative plan."

"Right," groaned Carl. "I could have sent everyone a new teleconference number 15 minutes before the meeting started."

"And keep in mind," I added, "that more and more people are logging in via wireless cards or home cable systems that aren't as fast or reliable as corporate Internet systems. That's why it makes sense to let them know that they should arrive 15 minutes early just to be safe."

"Everyone wins," reflected Iris. "They can work while they wait *and* the meeting starts smoothly, on time."

"Right," I agreed. "Now here are a few more virtual meeting disaster prevention tips:

✓ "**Disable distractions**. There are a remarkable number of potential distractions that can cause a virtual meeting to lose focus. Among them:

- ○ "**Email**. Disable pop-up reminders and incoming email dings.
- ○ **Screen saver**. Increase the time before your screen saver triggers.
- ○ "**Other phones**. Silence hard-line office phones and turn cell phones to vibrate.
- ○ "**Call waiting**. Virtual presenters should disable call waiting (usually *70) and/or forward calls to another phone. As Carl discovered, the beep of a call-waiting signal can be very distracting if you're presenting to a large group.
- ○ "**Instant messaging pop-ups**. Carl isn't alone. You need to disable these ahead of time. I had another client whose wife sent him an instant message that said *Hey Sexy, I can't wait to get my hands on you tonight!*"

"Awkward!" laughed Iris. "Well, Carl, I guess that tops Bob Gordon's colorful message."

"Not by bleeping much," said Carl with a self-deprecating laugh. He was starting to sound a bit less dejected as we talked. I continued:

○ **"Home office distractions**. Create a Quiet Please sign for your office door and use it during important meetings. Whenever possible, I recommend having a solid door that you can lock. However, if you don't have a door in your home office, you should discuss a hand signal that lets family members know when they must be quiet. Pets in the office are great company, but if they're loud—for example, a barking dog—I would recommend temporarily moving them out so you can sound more professional during the meeting. Speak to children about being quiet, and practice using your headset's mute function when interrupted by a loud surprise of any kind.

○ **"Meeting from the road**. If you're attending a virtual meeting from the road, try to find the quietest place possible. If you're in a hotel room, put up the Do Not Disturb sign on your door so the maid service won't interrupt you. If you have enough battery power, consider logging into web meetings from your safely parked car rather than a noisy restaurant or a hotel lobby with a weak Internet signal. It can eliminate background noise and interruptions. One warning about meeting in your car—be mindful that a parked car can get very hot or cold pretty quickly."

Iris said, "I'm starting to realize that some of our technical glitches were actually preventable. For example, I always arrive at web meetings at the last minute."

I paused to make an important point. "You're not alone, Iris. Many professionals now attend six or seven virtual meetings a week, but they've never been shown how to reduce technical problems."

"Until now," said Iris firmly. "What's next?"

✓ "Perform a sound, mute, and slide check.

- ○ "**Sound check**. Poor sound quality will cause meeting participants to tune out quickly. Ask a colleague if you're too loud, soft, muffled, or distorted *before* your guests arrive. Also check for hiss or static on the line. If there's a problem, hang up and call back in again. Then switch phones if the problem persists.

   "When the audio portion of a meeting is utilizing the Internet rather than a phone line, you should be extremely cautious. This technology, known as Voice over Internet Protocol (VoIP), can be highly effective, but there can also be major challenges. The VoIP line can be fuzzy, and many people do not understand that a headset is essential. Without a headset, the web broadcast could disturb other colleagues who work close by.

- ○ "**Mute check**. It's crucial to take a moment to review the Mute and Mute All functions before every meeting. A single participant who places the meeting on hold could force all 30 attendees to listen to cheesy 'on hold' music. Rapidly muting all can instantly solve this and other excessive noise problems while making you look like a pro.

"Other problems solved by the Mute function are noisy cell phones, background noise from airports or busy streets, unexpected office visitors, or loud pets."

"We recently had a large web conference in which our presenter forgot that the Mute All function was automatically turned on," moaned Iris. "Since the presenter couldn't hear the participants, he assumed the teleconference line wasn't working."

"Uh oh," I said. "What happened?"

"He started complaining about what he perceived to be a tech issue."

"So everyone heard what he said?"

"Every angry word came through loud and clear," groaned Iris.

"Ouch!" I said. "Here are two final things to check before your web meeting begins:

- ○ **"Slide check**. Run through all your presentation slides before participants arrive. In many cases you'll notice slides that need to be edited, removed, or hidden.

- ○ **"Access info check**. Make sure that presenter and participant sign-in information is clearly understood by all.

"You should also remember that practice makes perfect," I said. "So:

✓ **"Practice web maneuvers.**

- ○ **"Rehearse**. Practice all web conference maneuvers such as tossing control of the meeting to a colleague or visiting a website. This will uncover problems and build your confidence.

- ○ **"Test your web meeting survey tools**. If you're going to offer web conference survey questions, it's always smart to set up a mock question to test the survey tool and make sure it's working. Pick a fun multiple-choice question that can also serve as a pre-meeting icebreaker. For example: *What is the least productive part of your day: a) email, b) meetings, c) searching for info, d) phone calls, e) instant messaging, f) other?* A pre-meeting question sparks conversation while allowing you to test the survey feature."

I paused for a moment and then asked, "Are these insights helpful to you?"

"Yes," said Iris and Carl at the same time. Iris added, "But what about that echo thing? No amount of preparation could have prevented it from happening."

"True," I said. "That was a digital phenomenon called a hook flash, which occasionally occurs when someone hangs up and dials back in. When it happens to us, we dial a code. Then an operator comes on and does something that ends the problem."

"So I actually could have solved that problem," groaned Carl, "had I only known the code!"

"Right," I agreed. "Most disruptions can be remedied with a simple damage control strategy. The second half of the checklist will help you develop one."

Virtual Meeting Damage Control Checklist

✓ "Back up the presentation, teleconference, and presenter.

- ○ "**Back up the presentation**. If you're presenting a large slide presentation filled with graphics, create a backup PDF version that can be emailed in case you or a participant has a computer problem. A PDF is much smaller than a presentation in terms of megabytes."

"Makes sense," sighed Carl. "I could've sent it out in a flash."

"Here are some more backup strategies," I said.

○   **"Determine a backup teleconference number**. If the
    meeting's important, you may want to ask a colleague
    if you can use their teleconference number as a backup.
    This will allow you to quickly shift participants to a clean,
    working line.

○   **"Designate a backup presenter**. If the meeting is
    important, ask a colleague to be the backup presenter.
    Make sure they have presenter status within the web
    conferencing program. In the event you do experience
    problems, they can take over the presentation—"

"And save the day!" said Iris confidently. "We've never had
a backup plan. If I had been designated as a backup presenter, I
could have jumped in when Carl began having problems."

"Think of it as a new role that's arrived with the information
age," I replied. "Make sure that the backup presenter has a copy of
the presentation and understands what needs to be covered. Also:

✓ **"Have the teleconference and help center numbers on
    speed dial**. It's extremely stressful to get disconnected from
    a teleconference. One thing that will keep you focused
    and calm and get reconnected fast is to have your standard
    teleconference number on speed dial. It's also wise to have
    your help center number on speed dial.

✓ **"Create a technical difficulties slide**. If you are on a web
    conference and the teleconference system fails, it's very helpful
    to have a slide ready that addresses the problem." I showed
    them an example:

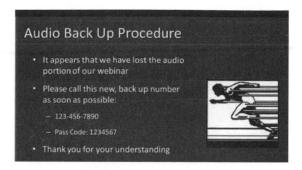

✓ **"Determine a secondary communication plan.** Cell phones can help you contact people who are late or missing from important virtual meetings. Since you may be using your hard-line office phone to attend the meeting, cell phone contact provides a secondary channel to discuss a meeting problem. If you get dropped from a teleconference line, you can call a colleague to see if they experienced the same problem."

"This happened last week!" cried Iris. "A key presenter from headquarters was late and no one had his cell phone number."

"Stressful?" I asked.

"Very," said Iris. "As it turned out, he had stepped out of his office and lost track of time. We left a message on his work line, but he didn't get it until after the meeting. Establishing cell phone as the fallback communication strategy would have saved that meeting."

I continued:

✓ **"Have a disaster recovery plan.** It's crucial to have a plan that helps you regain control after a technical glitch. In order for the plan to work, you need to know a little bit more about your virtual meeting technology. Here are a few great *what if* questions:

- ○ **"What if the leader gets disconnected from the teleconference?** Does everybody get dropped or just the leader?

- ○ **"What happens when the web conference organizer leaves the meeting?** Does everyone else get disconnected?

"Also:

✓ **"Smile and remain positive**. The panic you feel when a web meeting crashes is understandable. Remind yourself to remain positive and calm. Keep smiling, because when you frown or grimace it's reflected through your vocal tone, putting everyone on edge. Remember that if someone important is on the line, a technical disaster is a great way to demonstrate that you can handle tough situations."

"It's a great reminder," said Carl. "Showing my frustration won't increase sales. Next time, I'll keep smiling *and* I'll have a plan."

"And here's a final tip that will help you prevent technical problems and do a better job of reacting to them.

✓ **"Create a virtual meeting cheat sheet.** Develop a one-page quick-reference guide for your teleconference and web conference systems. Send it to everyone on your team. Be sure to include:

- ○ "Customer support contact info

- ○ "Account ID number

- ○ "Call-in number and passcode

- "Leader PIN
- "Participant PIN
- "Descriptions of how to use Mute and other features
- "Meeting recording instructions
- "Cost of using the service
- "Maximum participants allowed
- "How to rapidly sign in participants who have lost their access info
- "Etc.

"If you like, you can find a free download of a sample cheat sheet at the Info-Center at infoexcellence.com."

Iris said, "Thanks for this important second checklist, Coach. Every time I think you're going overboard, I remember all the problems we've had with virtual meetings."

"We now spend a fourth of our work lives in meetings,"[9] I responded. "We can't afford to waste it."

"It seems that many of these tips could also help my live meetings," said Carl. "For example, the concepts of Five Alive and having a backup plan are just as important in a live meeting."

"That's right," I said. "It's important to check on the LCD projector, food service, room temperature, and other elements of your live meetings."

"And now I have some good news," said Iris cautiously.

"You do?" I said with a smile.

"My boss, the global VP of sales, Penny Price, has reluctantly approved the final onsite Hamster Revolution meeting you requested. That means you can visit my team at Spex headquarters."

"Fantastic," I replied, wondering what Penny's reluctance was all about. "We'll cover staying on track and executing action items."

"There's one condition," said Iris, sounding concerned.

"Yes?"

"Penny wants to attend."

"Perfect," I said. "But I hear some concern in your voice."

"She can be pretty demanding, especially when she hasn't had her second cup of coffee. And I've found that she's a bit of a Hamster Revolution skeptic. I'm not sure why."

"Then we have something in common," I said with a smile. "I think a little skepticism is healthy. I'm confident we can show Penny the value of the revolution."

"I hope you're right," said Iris. "How about this deal: if Penny is really thrilled with the presentation, I'll buy you a cup of coffee at the Blue Sky Café in our building on the way out."

"It's a deal," I said. "But here's a warning: I plan to order a double mega-mochacinno."

"I think our budget can handle it," laughed Iris. "Bye, Coach."

"See ya, Coach," said Carl.

"Bye, Carl. Bye, Iris."

Your Hamster Revolution Assignment

Participants:

- Be prompt, prepared, and present at all virtual meetings. Avoid email and other distractions.

- Review virtual meeting checklists prior to the meetings.

- Arrive early and offer support when things go wrong.

Facilitators:

- Review both checklists for virtual meetings.

- For important meetings, review them twice!

11

STAYING THE COURSE

As I walked into the spacious, sun-soaked lobby of Spex Media, I felt excited to meet Iris' team. I knew from her emails that she was already seeing big productivity gains from our virtual meeting sessions. It didn't hurt that the caffeine from my mochacinno was just beginning to hit my bloodstream.

Iris' young assistant, David, greeted me in the lobby and escorted me to the conference room.

"We've seen a remarkable change in the past three weeks," said David as the regional managers and support team filed in well ahead of the 2:00 p.m. start time. David held up his PDA and smiled. "I've got the Objenda right here."

"Me too," said a new arrival dressed in a grey sports jacket. "I'm Vijay Patel, one of Iris' regional managers."

"And chief computer geek," said David with a grin. "Seriously though, Vijay's a genius at analyzing data, creating charts—all that tech stuff."

After quickly introducing me to a few more members of Iris' team, David pulled me aside. A look of concern flashed across his face. "Lately I've been worried about the change in Iris and now Pen—"

"Hey, David," said Iris as she entered the room, "I see you met the info coach. I hate to cut your conversation short, but you need to grab a seat because—"

"Five minutes early is the new on time," said a quiet voice behind me.

As I turned to see who it was, Iris said, "You two have met but not in person. Coach, this is Carl, your virtual meeting protégé."

Carl, a short, soft-spoken man of about 40, shook my hand and pulled me aside. "I was the first to pronounce this hamster stuff dead on arrival. But I have to admit our virtual meetings have improved dramatically. I've held two big webinars since we spoke and they both went great."

"It's working for us, too," said a well-dressed businesswoman wearing a stylish pair of designer glasses. "I'm Tasha Mathews, VP of marketing, and we really like the advertising concept that you and Iris developed. We've adopted Brainsurfing as a new way to rapidly generate ideas."

"Wonderful," I said, shaking Tasha's hand. "The meeting revolution has finally begun at Sp—"

"Nonsense!" said a loud but squeaky voice.

The entire room fell silent. Standing at the door, silhouetted by the sun, was another female hamster. Unlike Iris, this one seemed a bit angry, her paws crossed firmly in front of her dark brown business suit.

"We've tried to change meetings at Spex and it's impossible," she said, striding forward to shake my hand. "I'm Penny Price, the VP of global sales. And you must be the infamous info coach?"

"That's me," I said, stealing a glance at Iris, who looked nervous. "Nice to meet you."

There was an awkward pause and I felt obligated to address Penny's concerns.

"Penny, I understand that revolutionizing an organization's meeting culture isn't easy. But I believe that we're going to achieve a powerful, life-changing—"

"Cue the corny background music," said Penny, rolling her eyes and walking past me. "I just had to see how you and Iris propose to slay the meeting monster."

Penny took her seat and clapped her paws together. "Well, let's get the show on the road!"

Iris whispered, "I just found out that Penny spearheaded our last meeting initiative—the one that didn't go so well."

"Aha," I said. It was the first time I'd seen two hamsters in one room.

Iris started the meeting exactly at 2:00 p.m. She reviewed the Objenda, and then Carl did a wonderful job of introducing me to the team.

"Our first agenda item is keeping meetings on track," I began. "Can someone tell us about the last meeting you attended that went off course?"

Hands shot up around the room as team members shared their stories. Tasha, from marketing, recounted an end-of-the-day meeting that ran 40 minutes over, making everyone late for dinner. David talked about an 11:00 a.m. sales meeting that devolved into a commission debate.

"Meandering meetings usually run long," I said, adding, "they also slow down projects, performance, and eventually promotions."

"My concern," added Iris, glancing carefully at Penny, "is that *off course* meetings frequently fail to achieve their stated objective. This often leads to more meetings because the objective isn't attained."

The group groaned in agreement.

"What bugs me is when corporate mandates yet another rambling, national teleconference that runs long and further separates my sales people from their clients," complained Carl.

I nodded. "There are three keys to keeping meetings on track. First, we must elect an *Objenda Defender*."

"What's that?" asked Tasha.

Penny shook her head and crossed her arms. "It's just a fancy name for a meeting *timekeeper*, Tasha. Their job is to nag everybody to move on when a particular agenda item has taken too long."

"An Objenda Defender has a slightly more important role," I said gently. "In addition to watching the clock, they help to examine tangent topics that threaten to pull the meeting off course. Their job is to keep the meeting moving toward its stated objective. Sometimes the Objenda Defender's role is to *replace* an agenda item with a new one because it will bring the team closer to attaining the meeting's aim."

The entire room was silent. Everyone was looking at Penny. After a moment she sniffed, "Sounds like a timekeeper to me."

"Okay," I said, "the next thing we need is a simple question that the Objenda Defender can ask to begin the process of weeding out low-priority tangent items." I turned to the group. "When someone begins to drag a meeting off course, what do you do?"

"Fall asleep," said Vijay with a smile.

"Check my PDA for messages," said Carl. The group laughed.

Iris added, "I usually ask, *Is this issue a bit off topic?*"

Penny said, "I would say something like *Why are we talking about Project X when we're supposed to be talking about Project Z?*"

"Those are great questions," I agreed, "but the Objenda Defender's job is to ask one simple question relating to the meeting's stated objective." I walked to a flip chart and wrote:

Is the new topic more urgent and important than the other topics on the agenda?

David nodded. "That gets right to the heart of the matter."

"I like it," said Iris, "because it throws down a challenge to whoever brought up the new issue."

"Right," said Tasha. "Why replace something on the agenda with a topic that's less urgent and not as important?"

Iris leaned forward in her seat. "Now that we have an Objenda Defender armed with the urgent and important question, what's the final piece of the puzzle?"

"You need a simple tool that tells you what to do with each tangent topic," I replied as I began handing out copies of The Hamster Revolution for Meetings Power Tools card to everyone.

"Are you sure we need this?" protested Penny, who hadn't yet received her copy of the tool. Before I could answer, she asked, "I suppose you've come up with a snappy name for it?"

"NNNO," I replied.

"Well, that's good," said Penny flatly.

"*Actually*, that's the name of the tool," I said.

"It's called *Actually*?" asked Penny. "Not very imaginative."

"Whoops," I said with a smile, "I'm sorry for being unclear. The tool is called *NNNO*, and now that everyone has received their copy, let's take a look."

"Once the Objenda Defender asks if the tangent topic is more urgent and important, the group can use the NNNO tool to decide what to do with the issue."

David spoke up, "I get it. This is a simple four-box model that measures low to high importance and urgency. It tells you what you should and shouldn't be working on in a particular meeting."

"Perfect, David," I said with a grateful smile. "This tool can also help you prioritize other issues and events in your life. Let's take a look at each quadrant.

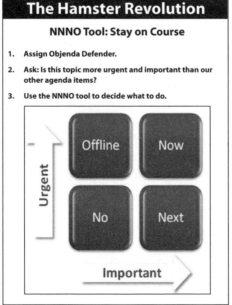

The Hamster Revolution

NNNO Tool: Stay on Course

1. Assign Objenda Defender.
2. Ask: Is this topic more urgent and important than our other agenda items?
3. Use the NNNO tool to decide what to do.

Urgent | Offline | Now
No | Next

Important

"**No = Less urgent and less important**: If the tangent topic is less urgent and less important than everything else on the agenda, say *No* to adding it to the meeting.

"**Next = Important but not urgent**: If the topic is important but not urgent, it should be discussed at the *Next* or a future meeting."

"Right topic but wrong meeting," said Penny flatly.

"Penny's right," I said, feeling relieved that she was participating.

"**Now = More urgent and more important**: If the topic is more urgent and more important than other agenda items—and it is clearly connected to the meeting's objective—then it's okay to cover it *Now* at this meeting. A big part of the Objenda Defender's role is to work with the group to find an agenda item that can be replaced by the new one.

"**Off-line = Urgent but not important**: If the topic is more urgent for one person but not important to the rest of the group, it's usually best to tackle it after the meeting or on a break. For example, if one or two people are having a problem with their benefits statement, it doesn't make sense for the other 20 people in the meeting to be involved in that particular discussion."

"But when we're frustrated, we sometimes push our issues into the meeting, making it hard to stay on course," noted Iris.

A murmur of agreement rose from the sales team.

Iris looked around the room and asked, "Is everyone willing to try:

1. "Assigning an Objenda Defender at your next meeting,

2. "Asking the Urgent/Important question,

3. "And using the NNNO tool?"

Her team responded with enthusiasm.

"No problem."

"Sure."

"Okay."

As their responses died down everyone noticed that Penny seemed to be thinking.

"Penny, how does this sound to you?" I asked.

She tapped her paws on the table and frowned. "I doubt this will work in the real world."

"A fair point," I said. "Let's use the real world as a test." I turned to the group and said, "Think about your last few meetings. Can anyone remember a non-agenda topic that was raised?"

"That's easy," said David with a grin. "Without naming names, one of our friends from marketing constantly brings up the issue of keeping gourmet coffee in the break room."

Laughter filled the room as several people looked knowingly at Tasha, who laughed and pointed at herself.

"Okay, Dave," she said with a grin, "so you want to mess with me?"

"Ah, yes," said Iris, laughing. "The gourmet coffee cost-benefit analysis discussion."

"Let's make Carl the Objenda Defender," I said, turning to Tasha. "Can you give us a 10-second description of your coffee concern?"

"I don't see why we can't order Blue Sky coffee and brew it ourselves," protested Tasha. "It would save everyone a lot of money."

Carl asked, "I understand Tasha's concern, but is gourmet coffee more urgent and important than our current agenda items?"

The group responded in unison, "No!"

Tasha smiled ruefully. "Okay, I'll admit that it's a bit of an obsession for me. Sue me for trying to cut costs!"

Carl turned to me and said, "So that's a *No*. Can anyone give us another example of a non-agenda topic?"

"I've got one," said Tasha. "Vijay, our data guru, took over last week's meeting and talked about some statistics that might be useful in the future. But those numbers won't be available for three months."

Several teammates nodded and Vijay smiled. "What can I say? I love crunching the numbers."

"Which category does this fall into?" asked Carl.

"*Next!*" was the loud response from everyone in the room except Penny.

Iris added, "It's good data, but you should put it on a future agenda and keep the meeting on track; it's important but not urgent."

"I've got one," said Vijay. "Does everyone remember when Iris left a bagel in the toaster oven, which set off the fire alarm during an important meeting? That certainly was *not* on the agenda!"

The group burst out laughing. Iris placed her head in her paws.

"Thanks for bringing up the burning bagel incident, Vijay," she said with a smile. "Remind me to discuss it at your next performance review."

Everyone laughed again and Carl raised his hand to quiet the crowd.

"Well," said Carl, "in addition to requesting Vijay's corner office once he's fired, I suppose we should ask if the burning bagel–fire alarm topic was more urgent and important than other agenda items on that day."

Tasha said, "I think it's a *Now* issue. A potential fire is a lot more urgent and important than anything on the agenda."

Nods all around indicated that the room was in full agreement.

Iris said, "Here's another one. When I'm running a meeting and someone has a computer problem, we often put things on hold and try to resolve the problem for that individual. I find that frustrating."

Carl smiled and stood up. "That's annoying. Why should one person hold up an entire meeting?"

He looked at the tool and asked, "Is this computer glitch issue more urgent and important than the other agenda items at a typical Spex meeting?"

Vijay raised his hand. "I think this problem is urgent for one person but not important to the overall team. According to the NNNO tool, topics like this are best handled off-line."

Carl addressed the group, "Does everyone agree?"

The group responded positively and Carl pointed to the *Off-line* section of this tool.

"This one's an O," he said with a smile.

Iris stood up and asked the group, "So does everyone feel as if they have a better way to keep meetings on track?"

"Yes!" was the quick response from everyone except Penny.

Iris continued, "Please implement the Hamster Revolution NNNO strategy at your next few meetings and provide feedback to me in two weeks. Okay?"

Everyone nodded and Vijay gave the thumbs-up sign. Penny flicked a bit of fur off her business suit. "According to the *Objenda*, you're also going to teach us how to get action items completed," she said quietly.

"I'll do my best, Penny," I said.

Your Hamster Revolution Assignment

Participants:

- Volunteer to be the Objenda Defender at one meeting this week.

- Consider your behavior in the past five meetings you've attended. How did you help or hurt the meeting's chances for staying on course?

- Use the NNNO tool to avoid pulling future meetings off course.

Facilitators:

- Assign an Objenda Defender for meetings that tend to stray off course.

- Ask the Urgent/Important question whenever possible and use NNNO to help the group decide what to do with non-agenda topics.

12

THE MEETING ACTION PLAN

"Raise your hand if you've recently attended a meeting where the action items didn't get completed on time."

A bunch of hands shot up.

"Why does that happen?"

"I think people get busy and they forget," said David.

"I always get this sinking feeling in the pit of my stomach," said Iris, "when I see people writing down their action items. I always wonder, *How can I make sure these things get done?*"

"Sometimes," said Vijay, "we don't even write them down."

"Do meeting notes always get sent?" I asked.

"Not always," replied Vijay with a sigh.

Penny protested, "The meetings that I facilitate always have complete meeting notes that get sent to every participant."

"And do you feel that your colleagues open the notes and act on the action items in them?" I asked gently.

There was a long pause and then Penny tore a blank piece of paper from her notepad, crumpled it up, and said, "I think half the time they do this with it—" She tossed the wadded paper through the air in a perfect arc and it dropped straight into a trash can on the far side of the room. Everyone burst out laughing.

"I used to play college basketball," she said with a wink.

"We need help!" exclaimed Iris.

I shook my head. "No, you need a *plan* that helps you capture and complete key action items."

The Hamster Revolution
Meeting Action Plan Tool

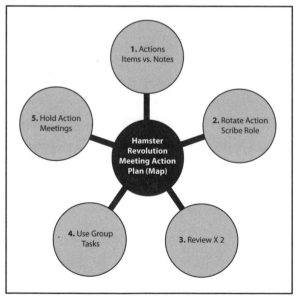

- 1. Actions Items vs. Notes
- 2. Rotate Action Scribe Role
- 3. Review X 2
- 4. Use Group Tasks
- 5. Hold Action Meetings

Hamster Revolution Meeting Action Plan (Map)

"A meeting action plan!" said Iris, pointing to the final tool on The Hamster Revolution for Meetings Power Tools card. "And step one is to focus on action items versus meeting notes."

Action Items Versus Meeting Notes

"I like that idea," said David. "I rarely have time to read through two pages of meeting notes."

"That's true," admitted Penny. "And the main reason we meet is to get things done—in other words, to take action."

"Terrific," I said. "So let's replace meeting notes with action items whenever possible. You may be surprised at how often a simple list of actions is all you need. Just make sure you designate *who does what when*."

Iris addressed the team. "Can we all commit to shifting from meeting notes to action items?"

Almost everyone nodded or said yes.

"I doubt that simply changing what you call something will make much of a difference," frowned Penny.

"Could it hurt to try?" I asked.

"I suppose not," she sniffed.

Rotate the Action Scribe Role

I looked around the room. "Who is recording the action items for *this* meeting?"

The room was silent.

"Well, duh," said Penny loudly, "everyone knows that we're supposed to pick someone to write them down."

Vijay chimed in, "I'll do it."

"Thanks, Vijay," I said earnestly. "And it's important to rotate the role of Action Scribe as much as possible. That way, everyone begins to take action items more seriously."

"Hmmm," said Iris thoughtfully. "When everyone's involved with reviewing and sending action items, it builds focus on meeting outcomes."

"It builds a sense of pride and ownership in team performance," I added with a smile. I turned to the group. "So here is some advice for the Action Scribe. Listen up, because someday it will be you.

- "Replace vague action statements like *One of us should take care of that* with clear and specific actions."

Vijay nodded. "Who's doing what when."

"Perfect," I replied.

- "Prompt your colleagues to remind you to put particular actions on the list in order to gain buy-in. For example, you might say, *Tasha, it sounds like you want to handle the logistics for the sales meeting. Should I add that to the Action Items list?*

"One final point," I said. "An actions list isn't very useful if you don't apply Review X 2."

"Another goofy term," said Penny icily as she rolled her eyes. I ignored that and continued.

Review X 2

"For recurring meetings, action items should be reviewed twice. First, at the end of the meeting, so that participants can openly commit to their proposed actions. This is an excellent opportunity for participants to add to, subtract from, or adjust their actions.

"The second review happens at the beginning of the next meeting. Knowing this open review will occur spurs team members to complete actions ahead of time."

"A little public humiliation goes a long way," laughed Tasha.

Iris joked, "We need every bit of motivation we can get, Tasha."

"In that case," said David, "how about a contest to see who can get the most action items completed in a month?"

"You mean an Action King?" asked Vijay.

"Or Queen!" said Tasha and Penny at once.

The room exploded in a chorus of contest ideas. Iris reined in the group by pointing at the clock and reminding them of our hard stop time. Carl used the NNNO tool to help the group see that this was an idea that could be added to the *Next* meeting agenda.

"I'll make that an action item for you," Vijay said to Iris. Everyone laughed. It was satisfying example of the Hamster Revolution in action.

Use Group Tasks

"Next topic," I announced. "How do you usually send out meeting notes?"

The room erupted with a single answer. "Email!"

"Why not use the Task function instead?"

The team looked puzzled and the room grew quiet.

Finally, David said, "Isn't that feature just for your own tasks?"

"Actually, most office productivity software allows you to assign a task to any individual or group you want," I replied.

David turned to Vijay, who was the only one with his computer open. "We can?"

Feeling the eyes of the entire room on him, Vijay stared down at his computer screen. "Okay, I'm creating a task and now I'm looking for—oh yes, here it is—*Assign Task*."

"Click on the Assign Task tab and select this team's distribution list," I said.

Vijay did the maneuver. Several people were standing up to peer over his shoulder. They looked surprised to learn that the Task function could be used for group distribution.

"Wow."

"That's new."

I noticed that Iris was looking very happy. She silently mouthed one word to me: "Cool."

"I get it," said Penny in a neutral tone of voice. "If we can assign our action items as a group task, then everyone, and I mean everyone, must accept that task. That builds accountability, and it provides a clear place where everyone can go to review their action items."

"And," said Iris, looking a bit surprised at Penny's positive response, "we can review each others' action items, too."

"Right," I said. "When I'm the Action Scribe I like to take down the actions inside a Meeting Power Draft. That way I can constantly review the Objenda while tracking the key actions."

"And that helps you coach participants as to what actions make sense based on the meeting's true purpose," said Carl with a grin. "I love that."

"Once I complete the list of actions, I simply cut and paste them into a Group Task. I set a completion date and shoot them to the team."

"And things get done," said Iris confidently.

"They do," I said. "Oh, and one more thing. I also try to ping people at the halfway point between the time the task was assigned and the time it's due. I've found that if you ping them too early, they ignore the message because the meeting is fresh in their minds. If you ping them right before the next meeting, they won't have time to react."

"So sending a reminder at the halfway point is just right?" asked Tasha.

"Exactly," I said. "So I create a pop-up reminder for the task for myself and then simply forward it to the team at the midway point."

Hold Action Meetings

"I see you have one more insight for us," said Penny, glancing at her card. "What are Action Meetings?"

"Action Meetings are all about completing team tasks *within* an actual meeting."

"You mean meetings where we actually *do* things instead of *talking* about doing them?" asked David with interest.

"Exactly," I replied. "There are a million different ways to apply the concept of Action Meetings. Here are just a few:

- "In a virtual web meeting, the facilitator can take team members to an intranet site where they can complete a form or key task. Some web conferencing systems actually provide active web pages that can be completed separately by each individual."

"Hold it!" said Vijay. "Let me confirm that we can do that."

He launched the Spex web conferencing tool and soon broke out in a big grin. "Yes. The presenter can take participants to an active web page that everyone can complete separately."

"Awesome," I said. "And that can help everyone complete a task before they leave the meeting.[10] Here are a few more Action Meeting strategies:

- "A leader can carve out 10 minutes at the end of each meeting for Action Sessions. In many cases a number of meeting participants will need to follow up with various members of the group. If this can be done in the meeting, it eliminates the need to waste time scheduling and reconvening at a later date.

- "If a large percentage of the team has fallen behind on a complicated task, time can be set aside for a walk-through from team members who have completed the assignment. This gets everyone over the finish line at the same time."

"The possibilities are endless," said Iris thoughtfully. She turned to Vijay and said, "I'd like everyone on my team to try an Action Meeting in the next month. Okay?"

Her entire team responded, "Yes!"

"Hold it," said Penny with a frown. "Doesn't that mean that we might be spending *more* time in meetings? Isn't the whole idea to spend less?"

"Not exactly," I said. "The idea is to meet less *and* get more done. So in some cases, extending a meeting by 15 minutes to complete a task that would take everyone half an hour…"

"Or force us to meet again in two weeks," said Vijay.

"…makes a lot of sense." I said, completing my thought.

There was an awkward silence as Penny thought this over. She looked as if she was about to protest but instead she simply said, "Okay."

You could almost hear a collective sigh of relief sweep through the room. All the meeting participants seemed energized and eager to implement their newly found Hamster Revolution meeting insights.

The meeting ended with Vijay reviewing the action items. He even held a brief Action Session with his colleagues to make sure that everyone knew how to create and distribute a group task.

Your Hamster Revolution Assignment

Participants:

- Volunteer to be the Action Scribe for at least one meeting this week.

- Review team tasks and see how you can help other teammates before the next meeting.

Facilitators:

- Rotate the role of Action Scribe.

- Use Review X 2 and have your Action Scribe send out the action list as a group task.

13

PENNY'S VERDICT

As everyone filed out of the meeting, Penny pulled Iris and me aside.

"I need to talk to you in private," she said.

As we walked briskly to her office, Penny was quiet. Iris shot me a worried look as we took our seats.

Penny hopped up in her chair and positioned herself carefully on top of three phone books. Iris, who had no phone books on her chair, had trouble seeing over Penny's large, oak desk.

Penny frowned, crossed her arms, and looked down at her notes.

"Well," she said cautiously, "I came in hating this rodent revolt. All these wacky terms and life-changing blah, blah, blah made this seem like a gimmick to me."

Iris gulped and winced at the same time. I tightened my grip on the arms of my chair. This was getting ugly.

Penny continued, "As you know, I've been trying to change meetings at Spex for 10 years without success. When Iris started talking about this hamster thing, I began asking lots of questions."

Penny gave me a stern look. "I checked your references and pumped Iris and her team for more info. And what I found…"

There was a long pause. Iris seemed to be bracing for bad news.

"I love."

"Excuse me?" asked Iris looking shocked. "What's that you said?"

"I love the Hamster Revolution," said Penny with a big smile. "It's exactly what we need."

"Tell, tell, tell us what changed your mind," stammered Iris sitting up in her seat and leaning forward.

Penny pointed to her Hamster Revolution for Meetings Power Tools card and said, "Each strategy makes sense:

1. **"Reduce meeting time**: I can only think of one group that wouldn't want us to reduce unnecessary meeting time: *our competition*.

2. **"Meeting Power Drafts**: David showed me his Meeting Power Draft today. No one has time to remember all the things that make a meeting great. You've automated it and now we can build it into our workflow.

3. **"The virtual meeting checklists**: Iris shared these with me. You've nailed our two biggest virtual meeting problems. 1) Our boring remote meetings are nothing more than glorified email sessions, and 2) we can barely turn our web conferencing system on without running into some kind of technical nightmare.

4. **"Staying on track**: I was *most* skeptical about this. I've been trying to keep meetings from veering off course for years. But the NNNO tool and Urgent/Important question make it fun and easy.

5. **"Completing action items**: You hit me right between the eyes with this one, Coach. It's my biggest peeve, and the Meeting Action Plan will definitely help us avoid project traffic jams and get more done."

Penny paused for effect and then smiled warmly. "Iris, I'll admit that I've seen a difference in your meetings, and your people are on fire for the Hamster Revolution. You've got my support for rolling this out in conjunction with Operation Elevation. Great job!"

As we left Penny's office I could see that Iris was on cloud nine.

"I believe I owe you a mega-mochacinno, Coach," she said.

"That's a *double* mega-mochacinno," I replied.

Over a delicious cup of coffee, Iris discussed her success with Penny and the importance of reaching her two Hamster Revolution goals. Compared to our first meeting on the plane, she was much more confident, energetic, and professional.

She paid our bill and we headed out into the sunny lobby of Spex Media. As I turned in my security badge, Iris let out a final sigh of satisfied relief.

"This was amazing," she said extending her paw for a handshake.

"Promise that you'll keep sharing the revolution, just like you did today?" I asked.

"Promise," said Iris with a smile. She turned and headed for the elevators that would take her back to her office.

Just before I reached the revolving doors, Iris called out, "Coach!"

I turned to see Iris on the other side of the lobby by the elevators.

"I won't let you down," she shouted, raising her tiny fist in the air just as she had on the plane. "Go hamsters!"

I raised my fist in solidarity, holding it there even as Iris disappeared into a sea of normal-sized people crowding into the elevator. The doors closed and Iris was gone.

EPILOGUE

WE MEET AGAIN

"I believe that's my seat next to you."

I looked up to see a tall, sharp-looking businesswoman dressed in a dark blue pants suit. She smiled intensely at me as if we shared some amazing secret.

"I'm sorry," I said, feeling confused. "Let me jump up so that you can—"

"Coach! Don't you recognize me? Don't you remember?"

"Uhhh," I bumbled, trying to place the face. *Who was this?*

"Spex Media?" she said raising her eyebrows. It was a clue.

"Iris?" I said slowly. "Is that you?"

"No! Definitely not!" she said, rolling her eyes and feigning sarcasm.

"Guess again!"

After a long, awkward pause it hit me.

"Penny? Penny Price?"

"Of course!" she said, mimicking a basketball player shooting a perfect jump shot.

"Great to see you, Penny. Of course I remember you."

As our flight prepared for takeoff, Penny brought me up to speed with Spex. The Hamster Revolution for Meetings had been a huge success.

"Thanks for providing those workshops and keynote talks to get things rolling," said Penny. "Having our executives attend the training was a brilliant idea. Suddenly they started arriving fashionably *early* for a change. And guess what?"

"What?" I asked.

"They're no longer spending the whole meeting doing the PDA prayer. We're getting a lot more done now that they're prompt and present."

Penny went on to relate how Spex had truly changed their meeting culture. The results were tremendous, with most colleagues saving 15 days a year.

"And what about Operation Elevation?" I asked.

"A big win for Spex," said Penny. "The pilot exceeded all goals, and even the stock analysts used it as an example of how Spex was cutting costs. Iris got a ton of recognition. She's up for a big promotion next month."

"And her family?" I asked, making a mental note to call Iris the next day.

"Well, as far as I know, everything's fine," said Penny thoughtfully. "She did say something about her girls making the semifinals."

"Was it soccer they were playing?"

"That's it!" said Penny, sitting up and beaming. "She's coaching them at soccer and they won a trophy. There's a picture on her desk."

"Awesome," I said, leaning back in my seat feeling satisfied.

Our plane accelerated down the runway and lifted off into the evening sky.

"I still can't believe the change we saw at Spex," said Penny slowly. "Once we jumped off the hamster wheel and pried open the bars of our meeting cages...we just...just..."

"Took off?" I asked with a grin.

"That's it," laughed Penny. "We took off."

RESOURCES

FAST ANSWERS FOR BUSY HAMSTERS

Over the next few months, Iris called several times to ask questions. What follows is a summary of those brief conversations.

■

IRIS: After a break, I sometimes have trouble getting people back on time. It's like herding hamsters! Is there a better way?

INFO COACH: Rather than saying, *Come back in ten minutes,* I recommend saying, *Everyone look at your cell phones. It's 10:41 right now. I need you back here in 10 minutes, which will be exactly 10:51 on your cell phone. Okay?* This way everyone is synchronized and the return time is concrete.

■

IRIS: Where can I go to find the desktop job aid, free tools, and information on Hamster Revolution training?

INFO COACH: Visit the Info-Center at www.infoexcellence.com.

IRIS: Some members of my team try to dominate the entire meeting. Others never say a word. How can I deal with all these difficult teammates?

INFO COACH: You need to tailor your approach to engage each team member. Here's a handy guide:

Description	Solution	Say...
The Dominator: Someone who frequently interrupts others and turns group discussions into speeches. In many cases, they want to be recognized as the smartest person in the room.	Summarize their position, thank them, and then firmly redirect the conversation so that all team members can contribute.	Ted feels we should try a different vendor and put the goals in writing. Thanks Ted. Now, Carrie has been checking the numbers and she has some interesting news for us. Carrie?
The Quiet One: A person who is shy and may feel that their opinion doesn't matter.	Give them a role that gets them talking early and makes them feel valued.	Hi, Manuel. Could you do us a huge favor today? Could you kick off the meeting with a review of your R&D idea? It's the best I've heard in a long time.
The Cycler: A meeting participant who likes to recycle a discussion point over and over again, making it hard to move through the agenda.	Establish a team mantra for this situation, like GEPO, which stands for Good Enough, Press On.	Folks, we seem to be in complete agreement on proposal X, so I'm going to say GEPO! Can we move to the next agenda item now?

Description	Solution	Say...
The PDA Prayer: Someone who spends half the meeting hunched over their PDA doing email.	Establish participation and TTO (Turn Technology Off) as ground rules. Call on the prayers frequently, and if it's a live meeting, walk around the room and stand behind them once in a while.	Before we start, I want to establish two ground rules: First, I want everyone to participate and provide input. Next I want you all to TTO. That means turn technology off and focus. Okay?
Dr. No: A person who is extremely negative.	Define the boundaries of their negativity in stark terms so that you can see where this person really stands on a topic. This often pressures them into a more realistic stance.	Nadine, it seems as if you have some legitimate concerns, and I'd like to clarify something. Are you saying that there's *no way* this project can succeed?

IRIS: Two of my teammates love to argue in our meetings. I'm tired of refereeing their disagreements. What should I do?

INFO COACH: Contrary to popular opinion, conflict can be a sign of a healthy meeting. Why meet if everyone agrees on everything? Disagreements build interest and force people to reexamine their positions. However, if the arguments are getting negative, overly time-consuming, or personal, I recommend talking to both participants separately off-line. Ask them to state their case. Listen carefully and then ask them to work together for the good of the team.

IRIS: What's the biggest mistake people make when meeting via videoconference?

INFO COACH: They forget to make eye contact. It's hard to connect with a person who's looking down during a video conversation or presentation. Remember to look directly into the camera and don't forget to smile.

IRIS: When I'm working on something that requires concentration, I sometimes lose track of time and forget about an important meeting. Any advice?

INFO COACH: In addition to setting computer reminders, you might want to try a sports watch with two alarm settings. Set the alarm to ring moments before your next two meetings. It works because although you can turn off a computer and put down your PDA, you normally don't take off your watch.

IRIS: When I run a web conference it's hard for me to record action items while also presenting. I would prefer not to write things down on a pad, because then I have to transfer them to my computer, which is time-consuming. Any advice?

INFO COACH: If you have a PDA, you might want to consider buying a foldable keyboard. I have found this useful in many situations where my laptop is being used for a live or virtual presentation. The keyboard is great because 1) it's faster than thumbing info into a PDA, 2) it's digital, so you won't need to transpose hard copy notes into a computer, and 3) it's low profile, so it works in some situations where opening a laptop might not be appropriate.

IRIS: We work with a foreign office. I'm forever messing up meeting times because of the different times zones. What should I do?

INFO COACH: You can add an additional time zone to your Outlook Calendar by going to Tools/Options/Preferences/ Calendar Options/Time Zone/Show Additional Time Zone.

IRIS: I have some colleagues who always click Tentative when I send them an e-calendar invitation. How can I get them to make a decision so that I will know who is actually coming to my meeting?

INFO COACH: Let invitees know that they must give a final answer by a concrete time and date. Also, explain to colleagues that tentative responses leave you in a bind and, in some cases, make it impossible to know if the right number of people will be at the meeting. If you select tentative on an invitation, be sure to indicate when you will confirm that you are coming. Here are a few more important e-calendar etiquette tips:

- If you decline an invitation, provide a reason.
- If you propose a new time, provide in the body of your message at least two other times that work for you.
- If your system allows, always check the availability of meeting participants before sending an invitation.
- If you work with an administrative assistant, spend five minutes a week discussing what kinds of meetings he should reject and accept.

IRIS: In the morning I find that I often get wrapped up in Outlook email before checking my calendar and planning my day. Sometimes I miss an important meeting or calendar item. Any advice?

INFO COACH: You can program Outlook to open up to your calendar first by going to Tools/Options/Other/Advanced Options/Start Up in This Folder: Calendar

IRIS: One of our clients uses a very basic web conferencing tool that has few interactive features. How can they make their meetings more interactive?

INFO COACH: Here are a few creative ways to engage participants without using advanced features like a survey. As a webinar facilitator, I have found that recording action items in plain view of a web audience builds interest because participants feel like they're getting a sneak peek at your inner thoughts and impressions. If chat and surveys aren't available you can also use the Raise Hand feature—which most web conferencing tools have—as a simple way to take a vote. Another feature that can be morphed into a voting tool is the mood indicator. I try to use a variety of notation features like a highlighter or pointer, which are available on almost every web conferencing tool. Occasionally, I will draw a smiley face or frown to make a point. Finally, I have found that simply playing music between breaks for live or virtual meetings builds interest. When the music goes off, people focus in.

IRIS: We're interested in upgrading our web conferencing system. Do you have any recommendations?

INFO COACH: We've created a handy review of key features that can be downloaded for free at the Info-Center at infoexcellence.com.

RESOURCES

CASE STUDY: CAPITAL ONE'S MEETING REVOLUTION

This case study underscores the value of implementing Hamster Revolution meeting insights across an organization. This case study and others like it can be found at www.infoexcellence.com.

I. SUMMARY

Challenge: **Capitol One** is an enterprise that constantly strives to maximize productivity. When internal surveys revealed that meeting overload was a growing productivity challenge for associates, Capital One's Productivity team took action.

Solution: The Capital One Productivity team partnered with Cohesive Knowledge Solutions, Inc., (CKS) to develop a ground-breaking meeting efficiency workshop. The program was based on CKS's **Info-Excellence® Get Control of Meetings seminar.** The training session delivered insights that reduced meeting time dramatically, saving over nine days a year per associate. Over 8,000 associates have since taken the training.

II. SITUATION

Capital One Financial (COF) has earned a sterling reputation for innovation, customer service, and leadership in the diversified financial services sector. Capital One manages over $100 billion in assets for 50 million customers worldwide.

Capital One's Productivity team isolated meetings as a major opportunity to increase productivity. Associates reported that low-value meetings were consuming more than 36 percent of their workday. Internal surveys reflected serious concerns about the quality and quantity of meetings.

III. ACTIONS

Capital One's Productivity team, led by Matt Koch, made the bold decision to design a meeting productivity training solution with the following principles in mind:

1. **Base the plan in data**: Partnering with Cohesive Knowledge Solutions, Capital One gathered as much information as possible via focus groups, surveys, external research, observation, etc.

2. **Customize and target the solution**: The workshop objectives were carefully tailored to reflect the exact needs of Capital One associates. Capital One survey data was incorporated into the workshop to gain added buy-in from participants.

3. **Fit the solution to the culture**: Capital One has a corporate culture that expects excellence while always doing the right thing by the customer, the associate, and the company. The workshop was designed to resonate with these core values.

4. **Apply intellectual rigor**: Actual results were measured carefully against workshop goals and a pre-intervention baseline survey in order to validate participants' 1.5-hour time investment in the meeting productivity workshop. Eighteen hundred surveys containing over 100,000 individual question responses were collected and analyzed during 2004–2005.

IV. RESULTS

Post-60-Day Survey Metrics: An analysis of post-60-day survey responses documented significant improvements in the value of meetings at Capital One. An average of nine days a year was saved by participants.

- **Meeting volume dropped by 13 percent**: Participants reported a reduction in meeting time of 13 percent. Reductions in meeting volume provided participants with the opportunity to reallocate 5 percent of their time to more productive activities.

- **Meeting quality improved by 38 percent**: Participants documented an impressive 38 percent increase in meeting quality. There was a 41 percent increase in the number of associates agreeing that most of the meetings they attend are efficiently run.

- **Leadership gains**: The workshop helped to empower associates to take control of the meeting environment via a new style of information coaching. Sixty days after training, the percentage of associates comfortable with meeting coaching had risen by 24 percent, to a total of 85 percent.

- **Post-One-Year Follow-Up Metrics**: Capital One and Cohesive Knowledge Solutions conducted a one-year post-training survey to determine if results could be sustained over time. The findings were extremely positive:
    - ○ 88 percent continued to leverage workshop best practices.
    - ○ 83 percent would recommend the workshop to all associates.
    - ○ 80 percent believed that the workshop made them more productive.
    - ○ 77 percent indicated that they continued to apply the coaching principles learned in the workshop.

V. CONCLUSION

The Capital One Productivity team did an excellent job of diagnosing and addressing two growing productivity challenges: ineffective meetings and meeting overload. They implemented a highly effective, breakthrough learning experience that resulted in major time savings, improved productivity, and a better work/life balance for associates. Results were sustained over one full year.

Download this and other case studies at www.infoexcellence.

Notes

1 Mike Song and Bill Kirwin, "Wounded Workflow: 4 Productivity Pain Points That Cost America a Trillion Dollars a Year"

2 Mike Song and Bill Kirwin, "Wounded Workflow: 4 Productivity Pain Points That Cost America a Trillion Dollars a Year"

3 Outlook users can select Categorize and the appropriate color. Then they can also select All Categories and create customized names for certain colors.

4 Meeting Power Drafts work in Outlook and Lotus Notes. Other email users can build templates by simply saving their draft into a standard folder or embedding a keyword that allows for a quick search retrieval of all power drafts.

5 Dr. William Glasser, Control Therapy in the Classroom, (New York: HarperCollins, 1986).

6 Karen Leland and Keith Bailey, Customer Service for Dummies (For Dummies, 2006), excerpted from "Like It or Not, Voice-Mail Is Here to Stay," Sterling Consulting Group, 2004 press release.

7 Find free images at http://office.microsoft.com/en-us/clipart/default.aspx

8 Some phone and web-conference systems will not allow you to get online 30 minutes early. In these situations, we recommend checking in with other presenters to review logistics.

9 Mike Song and Bill Kirwin, "Wounded Workflow: 4 Productivity Pain Points That Cost America a Trillion Dollars a Year"

10 Read our report on the five most underutilized web conferencing features at the Info-Center at www.infoexcellence.com.

Acknowledgements

The authors would like to thank the wonderful, amazing people who helped make our dream a reality. It's hard to believe that the revolution has come so far so fast. Thanks for believing. Special words of gratitude go out to:

Elena Song: Your brilliance helped us build a better hamster book, again.

Paul Ruane: Your insight and passion took this book to new heights.

Our publicity team: Thanks for all the amazing press. What are you going to do to top USA Today, WSJ, CNN, NPR, and GMA? Get us on 60 Minutes?

Major thanks to Rob Howe and the entire staff of People magazine.

Special thanks to our beloved publisher, Berrett-Koehler, including Steve Piersanti, Jeevan Sivasubramaniam, Mike Crowley, Maria Jesus Aguilo, Marina Cook, and many others. Writers take note: BK treats authors like gold.

A **super-duper big hamster hug** goes out to the CKS Core Team: Jeff Burress, Bill (2009 Wii Champion) Kirwin, Liza Rivera, and Kristin Song. We're so grateful for your talent, vision, and dedication to excellence. Without you, we're lost.

The entire Blanchard family, including Ken and Margie Blanchard, Tom McKee, Richard Andrews, Debbie Castro, Howard Farfel, Mark Forsyth, Romona Smith, Victoria Cutler, Jerry Acuna, Debbie Coolidge, and other amazing people such as Richard Anderson, Lisa Smedley, and Kate Orf, who contributed to the success of the Hamster Revolution. Thanks for opening doors we never could have opened ourselves.

Special thanks to Garrett Miller, Matt Koch, Paul Musico, and Tracey Campbell for your creativity, teamwork, and passion for performance.

We also wanted to recognize the entire worldwide network of Info-Excellence/Hamster Revolution trainers and sales partners. Thanks for joining the revolution!

The entire Song, Halsey, and Burress families, Hendrik Hynekamp, Teri Czudak, Ann Marie Sidman, Lisa Tabtabai, Petra Wynkoop, Beverly Tramontelli, Cheryl Strom, Adam and Michelle Raiti, Lisa Hiott, Bill Mallin, Craig Landau, Jeremy Springhorn, Dr. Flora Zaman, Sanjay Khanna, Ruth Aumick, Carol McGill, Betsy Meyers, Tom and Nancy Patton, Pam Wiggins, Frank (blue card) Getman, and info-hamsters around the world.

Index

Spinning your wheels on email?
Get a life!

1

CONFESSIONS OF AN INFO-HAMSTER

I was working peacefully in my office when the door slowly opened and shut with a click. I looked up but no one was there. "You'd better be able to help me!" said a small voice. *Was this a joke?*

I stood up and *that's* when I saw him. Trudging across the floor, tugging on his tie, was a small, nervous-looking white hamster with brown spots. He was wearing a dark blue business suit and carrying a small black briefcase. He looked tired and defeated.

"I hear you're the so-called productivity expert," he said. "I'm Harold."

I leaned down to shake his paw, "Pleased to meet you, Harold. And yes, my passion is helping professionals lead more productive and fulfilling lives."

Harold raised his eyes hopefully. "Maybe I'm in the right place after all," he muttered.

Once I'd gotten over my initial shock that Harold was a hamster, I realized that he was my 1:30 PM appointment.

"Welcome, Harold! Please sit down and tell me what brings you here."

Harold hopped into a chair facing my desk. As he leaned back, his wireless personal digital assistant (PDA) buzzed loudly. Harold looked down at it, lost his balance, and almost fell through the gap in the back of the chair. He scrambled frantically to keep from falling and eventually regained his composure.

"OK, OK. Here's my story. Five years ago I landed my dream job: Human Resources Director at Foster and Schrubb Financial. At first, the position was perfect. I was incredibly productive and my team launched several big initiatives." Harold frowned and shifted in his seat, "But a couple of years ago, I noticed that I was working harder and harder and getting less and less done."

"How'd that feel?"

"Am I in analysis or something?" quipped Harold, rolling his eyes. "Well, Dr. Freud, I felt stressed. I was getting buried alive by email, voice mail, and meeting notes: I had information coming out of my ears."

Harold pointed at the PDA clipped to his belt. "Then I got this thing. At first I liked being connected 24-7, but soon I fell even further behind and…"

"Yes?"

"To make matters worse," Harold said softly as he picked at some loose fur on his wrist, "and this is embarrassing to admit," he leaned forward and whispered, "Lately, I'm having trouble finding stuff."

I leaned forward and whispered, "What kind of *stuff*, Harold?"

"Well, I'll store an email and when I really need it — I can't find it! Things just vaporize! And don't get me started on my team's shared storage drive; everyone's storing documents differently; no one knows how to clean it up; it's a mess! I spend a lot of time requesting re-sends and re-creating documents that are missing. I'm staying late just to keep up."

"So work is spilling over into your personal life?"

Harold raised his furry eyebrows thoughtfully. He reached into his pocket and produced an impossibly small picture. I squinted and saw that it was Harold's family: a lovely wife and two beautiful children.

"Nice family."

"Upset family," corrected Harold wearily. "Thanks to wireless technology I'm always online. Carol's really frustrated with the amount of time I spend working after-hours."

He held up his paws with an exasperated look. "The kids hate it when I do email on Saturday or Sunday. But part of me actually looks forward to weekends just so I can catch up on work. Sometimes, I miss a soccer game or dance recital…but if I don't keep up…" Harold shrugged his little hamster shoulders as if to say *I just don't know anymore.*

"So your dream job's become a nightmare?"

Harold nodded. "I feel like I'm losing…me."

He continued quietly, "I used to love learning new things. I was thrilled to get to the office each morning. Now I dread it. I feel like… like…" Harold struggled for the right words.

"Like a hamster on a wheel?" I offered.

"Yes!" shouted Harold, bolting upright in his chair, "I've become a *hamster on a wheel!* Running faster and harder but getting nowhere."

I suddenly realized that Harold was unaware that he'd actually turned into a hamster. Although I'd helped countless professionals who felt and acted like hamsters, Harold was the first that actually *changed* into one! Apparently, his metamorphosis had been so gradual that he hadn't noticed.

Harold paused and let out a deep sigh. "When I was younger, I had a much different vision of how my life would unfold."

"Tell me about that."

Harold raised his eyebrows and stared at the ground. He looked like he was trying to recall a distant memory.

"Well, I dreamed I'd have this really fulfilling job. I pictured myself surrounded by brilliant people working on these high-level, high-impact team projects: Exciting stuff, life-changing stuff. I also imagined that I'd have much more time with my family, to laugh with friends…work out…garden…reflect…." Harold smiled wryly, "I never thought I'd spend every waking hour stressing over email and feeling like a hamster on a wheel."

2

A NEW WAY TO WORK

Harold raised his paws in frustration, "So you're the expert. How do I get off the wheel?"

"You fight back, Harold. There's a better way to work."

"Yeah, yeah," he said looking tense, "I've taken a couple time-management classes but they didn't help."

"Harold, this isn't a *time*-management problem…it's an *information*-management problem."

"It is?"

"Yes! Too much email and information is gushing into your life. Don't get me wrong: Email is an amazing communication tool. But suddenly, it's keeping a lot of people from getting things done. Most professionals feel like they're stuck on a nonstop wheel-of -information overwhelm."

"So what's the answer?" asked Harold, sounding frustrated.

"Join *The Hamster Revolution*."

"Huh?" asked Harold looking surprised. "Revolution against what?"

"Info-glut!" I said. "That's your enemy: way too much low-value information mucking up your world. You can't reach your fullest potential when you're drowning in email! *The Hamster Revolution* is a strategic plan that helps you conquer info-glut once and for all. Interested in learning more?"

"Sure," said Harold, looking both interested and worried at the same time.

I handed Harold a single sheet of paper, "Here's our schedule."

The Hamster Revolution Plan

Week 1 (Today): Email Insights (90 Minutes)
    Strategy 1: Reduce email volume
    Strategy 2: Improve email quality
    Strategy 3: Coach others to send you more actionable email

Week 2: Information Storage Insights (60 Minutes)
    Strategy 4: File and find info fast with COTA

Week 3: Wrap-Up Meeting (30 Minutes)

Harold studied the schedule and seemed pleased, "Three hours works for me. I don't have a lot of time for this."

I nodded, "Today, we'll focus on streamlining the flow of email through your life. This will help you become more relaxed and effective at work. Sound good?"

"Wonderful, if I could actually do it," replied Harold cautiously.

"Don't worry. Our goal today is to concentrate on a *small* number of *high-impact* email insights. By the way, you won't have to write anything down because each Hamster Revolution strategy will be summarized by an easy-to-use tool."

"Four strategies and four tools…that's good," stated Harold emphatically. "But what exactly is next week's meeting about? What is COTA?"

"A moment ago you mentioned that you were having trouble finding things?"

"Sure."

"What if you could file and find all of your email, documents, and links in a flash?"

"That would be a miracle," said Harold softly.

"I can't promise you a miracle, but I've seen amazing results from people who've adopted an organizational system called COTA. COTA is a simple yet effective way to arrange your files and folders. After the COTA session, we'll give you a week to put all four strategies into practice on the job. During that week, you can call me anytime for coaching or feedback. OK?"

Harold thought for a moment, "Seems like a workable plan—so far."

We'll hold a third and final wrap-up meeting to see how you did. We can fine-tune your newly found Hamster Revolution skills and answer any lingering questions."

Harold leaned forward, "So it's kind of like a one-two punch? First we get email under control and then we use this COTA thing to organize my information?"

I nodded, "We've discovered that there's a powerful *connection* between email efficiency and the way you store your info."

"What kind of connection?"

"Here are just a few examples:

- Reduced email volume means less email to store.

- Clear email subject lines make it easier to relocate stored email.

- A highly effective folder system helps you rapidly file email and documents. This reduces inbox overload.

- Responding to an email requesting info is a lot easier when you can find your info fast.

- There's also a time connection. Together, email and information storage tasks consume over 40% of a typical professional's day. [1] [2] When both of these activities become more efficient, your overall productivity takes a giant leap forward."

Harold raised his eyebrows, "So I need to improve *both* email and information storage to get off the hamster wheel?"

I nodded, "We're going to get your life back, Harold."

"I'll believe it when I see it," said Harold. "But I like your approach. You're looking at the whole process of managing information, not just email by itself. I've never thought of it that way before."

"You're not alone. Most professionals lack an effective plan for managing all the information flooding into their lives. To make matters worse, over the past five years the volume of information we process has skyrocketed. For example, email volume is rising at a rate of 14.6% per year." [3]

Harold groaned, "I'm doomed."

"As inboxes and computer filing systems have become bloated, millions of professionals have begun to feel like hamsters. *Well, it's time for the hamsters to fight back*! The Hamster Revolution will restore order and control to your life. Best of all, it will save you 15 days a year."

Harold looked surprised, "15 days?"

"You can save a lot of time by mastering the flow of information through your world. So what do you think?"

Harold reflected on his predicament for a moment. Suddenly, with a determined look, he blurted, "OK, I'll join your Hamster Revolution!"

"*Our* revolution," I smiled, "ready to reclaim your life?"

Harold stood up on his chair and gave a mock salute, "Let the revolting begin!"

....

Visit the Info-Center at www.infoexcellence.com/ch3.htm to read chapter 3 and purchase copies of both Hamster Revolution books at a specially discounted rate.

About the Authors

Mike Song: ms@infoexcellence.com

Mike Song is one of the world's leading productivity speakers. His popular Get Control keynote speeches for email, Blackberry®, and meetings are filled with life-changing insights, practical advice, and hilarious activities. Participants save time—over 15 days a year—while getting more done.

Mike has appeared on CNN, Good Morning America, NPR, and CNBC. He is coauthor of The Hamster Revolution: How to Manage Your Email Before It Manages You (Berrett-Koehler, 2008), a best-seller with over 125,000 copies in print in 11 languages. Mike is CEO of Cohesive Knowledge Solutions, Inc. His clients include Gen Re, Boeing, Novartis, United Technologies, Time Inc., and the Public Broadcasting Service.

He lives in Connecticut with his wife, Kristin, and children Emily, Evan, and Ethan.

Vicki Halsey Ph.D.: vicki.halsey@kenblanchard.com

Vicki Halsey is the vice president of Applied Learning for the Ken Blanchard Companies. She is a valued presenter, keynote speaker, consultant, coach, author, and trainer, who also teaches in and designed the Master of Science in Executive Leadership (MSEL) program at the University of San Diego and the Executive MBA program at Grand Canyon University. Vicki's expertise in optimal learning strategies, leadership, and blended solutions come together as she designs and delivers innovative, high-impact leadership, team, and customer service programs. Her passion is helping professionals regain balance and meaning in their lives so they can return home from work happy and ready to enrich the lives of their families. A partial list of Vicki's clients includes Microsoft, Nike, Oracle, ADP, KPMG, Nokia, Toyota, NBA, Pfizer, GAP, Merrill Lynch, Wells Fargo, Gillette, and Procter & Gamble. Vicki lives in San Diego with her two sons and husband/author, Rick.

Timothy Burress: tb@infoexcellence.com

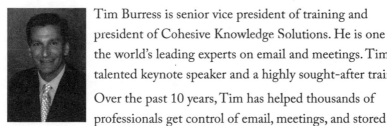

Tim Burress is senior vice president of training and president of Cohesive Knowledge Solutions. He is one of the world's leading experts on email and meetings. Tim is a talented keynote speaker and a highly sought-after trainer.

Over the past 10 years, Tim has helped thousands of professionals get control of email, meetings, and stored information. He co-developed the acclaimed Info-Excellence productivity seminar. He is a coauthor of The Hamster Revolution: How to Manage Your Email Before It Manages You (Berrett-Koehler, 2008), a best-seller with over 125,000 copies in print in 11 languages. Tim's clients include Capital One, Procter & Gamble, Hewlett-Packard, McDonalds, and Mercedes-Benz. Tim lives in Virginia with his wife, Daphne, and daughters Grace and Ava.

SERVICES AVAILABLE

The Ken Blanchard Companies are global leaders in workplace learning, productivity, performance, and leadership effectiveness solutions. We help companies improve their performance, productivity, and bottom-line results. Blanchard solutions are based on the belief that people are the key to accomplishing strategic objectives and driving business results. These solutions develop excellence in leadership, employee engagement, team building, customer loyalty, organizational change, and performance improvement. The companies' continual research points to best practices for workplace improvement. Their world-class trainers and coaches drive organizational and behavioral change at all levels and help people make the shift from learning to doing.

Blanchard's integrated approach to better organizational performance provides a common system, framework, and language at every level of your organization. The practicality and simplicity of our Situational Leadership® II model has made it one of the most widely adopted leadership processes in the world.

Contact us to learn more about the results we have delivered for other organizations and to identify the options that best meet your needs.

Global headquarters:
The Ken Blanchard Companies
125 State Place
Escondido CA 92029
www.kenblanchard.com
1-800-728-6000 in the U.S.
1-760-489-5005 from anywhere

About Berrett-Koehler Publishers

Berrett-Koehler is an independent publisher dedicated to an ambitious mission: Creating a World That Works for All.

We believe that to truly create a better world, action is needed at all levels—individual, organizational, and societal. At the individual level, our publications help people align their lives with their values and with their aspirations for a better world. At the organizational level, our publications promote progressive leadership and management practices, socially responsible approaches to business, and humane and effective organizations. At the societal level, our publications advance social and economic justice, shared prosperity, sustainability, and new solutions to national and global issues.

A major theme of our publications is "Opening Up New Space." They challenge conventional thinking, introduce new ideas, and foster positive change. Their common quest is changing the underlying beliefs, mindsets, institutions, and structures that keep generating the same cycles of problems, no matter who our leaders are or what improvement programs we adopt.

We strive to practice what we preach—to operate our publishing company in line with the ideas in our books. At the core of our approach is stewardship, which we define as a deep sense of responsibility to administer the company for the benefit of all of our "stakeholder" groups: authors, customers, employees, investors, service providers, and the communities and environment around us.

We are grateful to the thousands of readers, authors, and other friends of the company who consider themselves to be part of the "BK Community." We hope that you, too, will join us in our mission.

Be Connected

Visit Our Website

Go to www.bkconnection.com to read exclusive previews and excerpts of new books, find detailed information on all Berrett-Koehler titles and authors, browse subject-area libraries of books, and get special discounts.

Subscribe to Our Free E-Newsletter

Be the first to hear about new publications, special discount offers, exclusive articles, news about bestsellers, and more! Get on the list for our free e-newsletter by going to www.bkconnection.com.

Get Quantity Discounts

Berrett-Koehler books are available at quantity discounts for orders of ten or more copies. Please call us toll-free at (800) 929-2929 or email us at bkp.orders@aidcvt.com.

Host a Reading Group

For tips on how to form and carry on a book reading group in your workplace or community, see our website at www.bkconnection.com.

Join the BK Community

Thousands of readers of our books have become part of the "BK Community" by participating in events featuring our authors, reviewing draft manuscripts of forthcoming books, spreading the word about their favorite books, and supporting our publishing program in other ways. If you would like to join the BK Community, please contact us at bkcommunity@bkpub.com.